Standards for Middle and High School Literacy Coaches

International Reading Association
in collaboration with
National Council of Teachers of English
National Council of Teachers of Mathematics
National Science Teachers Association
National Council for the Social Studies

INTERNATIONAL
Reading Association
800 BARKSDALE ROAD, PO BOX 8139
NEWARK, DE 19714-8139, USA
www.reading.org

Literacy Coach Standards Team Members

Peggy Altoff	National Council for the Social Studies, Silver Spring, MD
Judy Buchanan	National Writing Project, Berkeley, CA
Douglas Buehl	Madison Metropolitan Schools, Madison, WI
Marguerite Carlucci	Westport Public Schools, Westport, CT
Diane DeFord	University of South Carolina, Columbia, SC
Rowena Douglas	National Science Teachers Association, Arlington, VA
Kathryn Egawa	National Council of Teachers of English, Urbana, IL
Alan Farstrup	International Reading Association, Newark, DE
Susan Griffin	National Council for the Social Studies, Silver Spring, MD
Brian Hand	University of Iowa, Iowa City, IA
Evelyn Hanssen	Aurora Public Schools, Aurora, CO
Carol Issacs	Fairfax County Public Schools, Fairfax, VA
Michael Kamil	Stanford University, Palo Alto, CA
Barbara Kapinus	National Education Association, Washington, DC
Jim Knight	University of Kansas, Lawrence, KS
Rich Long	International Reading Association, Newark, DE
Shirley McCann	Literacy Consultant, Reston, VA
Elizabeth Moje	University of Michigan, Ann Arbor, MI
Chris Pratt-Consotelli	Harris County Schools, Hamilton, GA
Cathy Roller	International Reading Association, Newark, DE
Jim Rubillo	National Council of Teachers of Mathematics, Reston, VA
Deborah Short	Center for Applied Linguistics, Washington, DC
Elizabeth Sturtevant	George Mason University, Arlington, VA
Emma Trevino	Charles A. Dana Center, University of Texas, Austin, TX
MaryEllen Vogt	International Reading Association, Newark, DE
Kent Williamson	National Council of Teachers of English, Urbana, IL
Gene Zablotney	Fairfax County Public Schools, Fairfax, VA

Carnegie Corporation's *Advancing Literacy* program is dedicated to the issues of adolescent literacy and the research, policy, and practice that focuses on the reading and writing competencies of middle and high school students. *Advancing Literacy* reports and other publications are designed to encourage local and national discussion, explore promising ideas, and incubate models of practice, but do not necessarily represent the recommendations of the Corporation. For more information visit www.carnegie.org.

Published by the International Reading Association.

Suggested citation: International Reading Association. (2006). *Standards for middle and high school literacy coaches*. Newark, DE: Author.

Library of Congress Cataloging-in-Publication Data
Standards for middle and high school literacy coaches / International Reading Association in collaboration with National Council of Teachers of English ... [et al.].
    p. cm.
Includes bibliographical references.
ISBN 0-87207-597-4
    1. Content area reading--United States. 2. Reading (Middle school)--United States--Standards. 3. Reading (Secondary)--United States--Standards. I. International Reading Association. II. National Council of Teachers of English.
    LB1050.455.S734 2005
    428.4071'2--dc22

2005029314

Contents

Acknowledgments

Many staff and members from the partner organizations the International Reading Association, the National Council of Teachers of English, the National Council of Teachers of Mathematics, the National Science Teachers Association, and the National Council for the Social Studies took part in the formulation of the *Standards for Middle and High School Literacy Coaches*. Without their tireless efforts, this guide would not have been possible. In particular, we owe a debt of gratitude to Cathy Roller from the International Reading Association for her constant encouragement, advice, and leadership in this effort.

We pay special tribute to Carnegie Corporation of New York for its generous support and specifically to Andrés Henríquez for helping to launch this effort and for his inspired guidance and feedback throughout the development process. Thanks to Susan Pimentel, standards expert and analyst, for her keen writing and editorial skills. Her ability to deal with large numbers of people and focus on the task was masterful. We also extend our appreciation to Catherine Snow and Robert Schwartz, Harvard Graduate School of Education; Michael Kamil, Stanford University; and doctoral student extraordinaire Gina Biancarosa, Harvard Graduate School of Education. Thanks also to Center for Applied Linguistics expert Deborah Short, whose observations and suggestions on English-language learners were invaluable.

Finally we express our gratitude to the many literacy coaches who provided precious insight into what skills and knowledge are necessary to be effective and who ensured that our work stayed grounded in reality. Special thanks to our panel of coaches: Jacy Ippolito, Baldwin School, Cambridge, MA; Cathleen Kral, Boston Public Schools; Evan Lefsky, Just Read! Florida!; Michele McClendon, Pittsburgh Public Schools; and Dennis Szymkowiak, Mundelein High School, Mundelein, IL.

Carnegie Corporation of New York

Carnegie Corporation of New York was created by Andrew Carnegie in 1911 to promote the advancement and diffusion of knowledge and understanding. As a grantmaking foundation, the Corporation seeks to carry out Carnegie's vision of philanthropy, which he said should aim "to do real and permanent good in the world." The Corporation's capital fund, originally donated at a value of about $135 million, had a market value of $1.9 billion on September 30, 2004. The Corporation awards grants totaling approximately $80 million a year in the areas of education, international peace and security, international development, and strengthening U.S. democracy.

About the Collaborators

International Reading Association

The International Reading Association is a professional membership organization that promotes high levels of literacy for all by improving the quality of reading instruction, disseminating research and information about reading, and encouraging a lifetime reading habit. IRA's 80,000 members include classroom teachers, reading specialists, consultants, administrators, supervisors, university faculty, researchers, psychologists, librarians, media specialists, and parents. IRA affiliates with reading organizations in 99 countries, extending its network to more than 300,000 people worldwide.

National Council of Teachers of English

The National Council of Teachers of English, with 60,000 individual and institutional members worldwide, is dedicated to improving the teaching and learning of English and the language arts at all levels of education. For more information, please visit www.ncte.org.

National Council of Teachers of Mathematics

The National Council of Teachers of Mathematics is a public voice of mathematics education, providing vision, leadership, and professional development to support teachers in ensuring mathematics learning of the highest quality for all students. With 100,000 members and 250 affiliates, NCTM is the world's largest organization dedicated to improving mathematics education pre-K–12. The Council's *Principles and Standards for School Mathematics* includes guidelines for excellence in mathematics education and issues a call for all students to engage in more challenging mathematics. NCTM is dedicated to ongoing dialogue and constructive discussion with all stakeholders about what is best for U.S. students.

National Science Teachers Association

The National Science Teachers Association, founded in 1944 and headquartered in Arlington, Virginia, is the largest organization in the world committed to promoting excellence and innovation in science teaching and learning for all. NSTA's current membership of more than 55,000 includes science teachers, science supervisors, administrators, scientists, business and industry representatives, and others involved in and committed to science education.

National Council for the Social Studies 🌐 NCSS

Founded in 1921, National Council for the Social Studies is the largest association in the United States devoted solely to social studies education. NCSS defines *social studies* as "the integrated study of the social sciences and humanities to promote civic competence." Its membership of 26,000 individuals and institutions is organized into a network of more than 110 affiliated local, state, and regional councils and associated groups composed of pre-K–12 classroom teachers, college and university professors, school officials, supervisors and consultants, publishers, and other social studies professionals. Social studies educators teach students the content knowledge, intellectual skills, and civic values necessary for fulfilling the duties of citizenship in a participatory democracy. The mission of NCSS is to provide leadership, service, and support for all social studies educators.

Introduction

Every school day in the United States for the past decade, more than 3,000 students drop out of high school (Joftus, 2002). Most are unable to keep pace with the rigors of the curriculum. They simply do not have the literacy skills to make sense of their textbooks (Allington, 1994; Kamil, 2003).

In years past, literacy was limited to the ability to read and understand a simple document and write one's name on a contract. Literacy demands in today's workplace have accelerated. High school graduates are required to interpret a wide range of reference materials: journal articles, memoranda, and other documents that may contain technical information, including intricate charts and graphs. Increasingly, they are expected to judge the credibility of sources, evaluate arguments, develop and defend their own conclusions, and convey complex information in ways that will either advance scholarship in a discipline or contribute to workplace productivity—skills well beyond the reach of poor readers.

> "In a world constructed around the assumption that everyone has the basic skills of literacy and where literacy and freedom are indissolubly linked, to be illiterate is to be unfree."
>
> —KOICHIRO MATSUURA, Director-General of UNESCO, on International Literacy Day (September 8, 2002)

The number of secondary school students who lack literacy skills is not inconsequential: Over 6 million U.S. students in grades 8–12 are struggling readers (Joftus, 2002). One in four adolescents cannot read well enough to identify the main idea in a passage or to understand informational text (Kamil, 2003). ACT, a leading producer of college admission tests, reports that approximately 50% of high school graduates in 2005 did not have the reading skills they needed to succeed in college (Arenson, 2005). Without targeted literacy instruction, many who graduate from high school will be ill-equipped for the demands of college or the new economy, relegated to remedial courses or dead-end jobs (American Diploma Project, 2004). Results from ACT's WorkKeys program—an assessment of foundational skills for workplace success—indicate that young people need reading skills comparable to those of college freshmen in order to secure jobs that pay more than minimum wage but don't require a four-year college degree (ACT, 2003).

What Adolescents Need

Much of the nation's attention and hundreds of millions of dollars in funding has been focused on early reading instruction targeted to the primary grades. But children who are reading up to grade level in the primary grades do not automatically become proficient readers in later grades (Biancarosa & Snow, 2004). Many have difficulty transitioning from the children's stories they read in the early grades to more complex content area textbooks in middle and high school (Sturtevant, 2003). Moreover, national longitudinal data show that three quarters of students who exit third grade as struggling readers continue to read poorly in high school (Peterson, Caverly, Nicholson, O'Neal, & Cusenbary, 2001; RAND Reading Study Group, 2002). In addition, demographic analyses confirm a significant influx of immigrants whose native language is not English into the U.S. civic fabric. These students enter schooling at all levels, including middle and high school.

As literacy problems of older students gain traction with education policymakers, the view that literacy is the domain of primary educators and is only addressed in secondary school as a remedial subject has given way to a more enlightened view that to fix underachieving middle and high schools in the United States, secondary teachers nationwide need to confront the poor reading skills of their students. (Though the term *secondary* is informally taken to refer to high schools, we use it in its more technical meaning, referring to the post-primary grades, including middle school grades.) There is a solid body of knowledge on adolescent literacy, so experts know what to do: Faculty members need to become teachers of reading and writing appropriate to their disciplines. Although many middle and high school teachers understand the importance of literacy, they do not automatically see its instruction as their job. Resistance to reading instruction in the content areas dates back over 60 years (Artley, 1944). Tradition says that teaching reading is the job of primary school teachers. Complicating matters, content area teachers rarely have expertise in teaching literacy: Most preservice programs for secondary school teachers only require one content area reading course. Facing considerable pressure to cover content for state assessments, content area teachers also worry that teaching literacy takes essential time away from teaching their subject matter.

> "This is an extremely complex problem, and the longer we let these kids go the more serious the problem becomes. The problem exists because [after 3rd grade] we stop providing reading instruction, and the instruction we do provide is not what they need."
>
> —MICHAEL KAMIL (as cited in Manzo, 2005, p. 38)

Middle and high school teachers need help to understand how they can develop content knowledge at the same time that they improve student literacy; that in fact, effective teaching in their subject areas will be boosted by complementary literacy instruction related to the texts (and the other communication demands) characteristic of their subjects. Plenty of data exists in school districts across the United States to show that teachers who infuse these techniques into their classes are able to cover (and their students are able to learn) more content more successfully. At J.E.B. Stuart High School in Falls Church, Virginia, for example, 76% of students had been reading below grade level before the principal instituted a literacy program. Today, the school is recognized as a "breakthrough high school": Only a small number of its students are behind (National Association of Secondary School Principals [NASSP], 2005). In South Salt Lake City, Utah, staff at Granite Park Middle School credit the school's literacy program with turning around its mathematics and science scores—once the lowest in the district. Several years after instituting a literacy program, Cedar Ridge Middle School in Decatur, Alabama, has seen its writing scores improve sharply (McGrath, 2005). Reading achievement has improved there as well. A literacy immersion action plan at Hopkins West Junior High in Minnetonka, Minnesota, has helped to close the achievement gap (NASSP, 2005).

Current practice suggests a promising avenue for intervention that includes qualifying literacy experts to coach content area teachers in the upper grades who currently lack the capacity and confidence (and sometimes the drive) to teach reading strategies to students particular to their disciplines. While there are few studies—and no systematic body of research—reporting on the direct link of literacy coaching to student learning, as noted above, schools that have adopted this approach report remarkable improvements.

The logic is compelling. Inservice provided to teachers results in improved reading achievement for students (National Institute of Child Health and Human Development

[NICHD], 2000). So it follows naturally that literacy coaching—a form of highly targeted professional development—is a particularly potent vehicle for improving reading skills. Literacy coaching adheres to what research identifies as the essential features of effective professional development (Darling-Hammond & McLaughlin, 1995; Garet, Porter, Desimone, Birman, & Yoon, 2001). Common components include training that is

- grounded in inquiry and reflection
- participant-driven and collaborative, involving a sharing of knowledge among teachers within communities of practice
- sustained, ongoing, and intensive
- connected to and derived from teachers' ongoing work with their students

Professional development, delivered as sustained, job-embedded coaching, maximizes the likelihood that teachers will translate newly learned skills and strategies into practice (Joyce & Showers, 1996; Neufeld & Roper, 2003).

Developing the Standards

Adolescent literacy has become a major aim of a number of public and private initiatives in the United States. President Bush's Striving Readers program has dedicated $25 million for fiscal year 2005 to research-based school-based programs with Congress expected to award $30 to $35 million for fiscal year 2006. In a tight budget year, this program has received an increase in funding, illustrating the priority the President and Congress place on adolescent literacy. Two other pieces of legislation have been proposed in Congress to improve U.S. high schools by funding adolescent literacy programs: the PASS Act (S.1061) and Graduation for All Act (H.R. 547). The U.S. Department of Education, in partnership with NICHD, has issued grants to a network of five adolescent literacy experts around the nation to improve knowledge in the field, and it has made grants to schools in order to study the impact of adolescent literacy programs on struggling ninth-grade readers in smaller learning communities. Private foundation initiatives abound as well. With millions of dollars and students' school success on the line, *Standards for Middle and High School Literacy Coaches* is meant to stiffen the resolve of education policymakers and schools that embrace coaching to do so mindfully, so this reform will not go the way of so many good intentions and produce minimal results.

"Research shows...that students who receive intensive, focused literacy instruction and tutoring will graduate from high school and attend college in significantly greater numbers than those not receiving such attention. Despite these findings, few middle or high schools have a comprehensive approach to teaching literacy across the curriculum.... Students require teachers who are knowledgeable in the subject they teach and can convey the subject matter effectively."

—SCOTT JOFTUS (2002, p. 9)

Key disciplinary organizations representing secondary school teachers pooled their talents to specify what literacy coaches must know and be able to do to function effectively to train faculty in literacy techniques. This historic partnering includes the International Reading Association (IRA), National Council of Teachers of English (NCTE), National Council of Teachers of Mathematics (NCTM), National Science Teachers Association (NSTA), and National Council for the Social Studies (NCSS).

The collaborators spent nearly a year and a half gathering empirical evidence to codify the knowledge and skills that secondary school literacy coaches need to exhibit in order to be effective. With support from Carnegie Corporation of New York, representatives from the five organizations gathered in May 2004 to forge the "must have" competencies for literacy coaches. During that session, they agreed on format and set the parameters for the development of literacy coach standards. Thereafter, panels from each organization worked to build a set of standards appropriate to its content area. Four months later, the organizations reconvened to review one another's drafts and grapple with the issue of how best to combine the distinct organization standards into a comprehensive set of draft standards for middle and high school coaches. The draft expectations that resulted from that meeting represented more than a merging of four discrete documents. Common ground was forged, although important differences particular to the demands of each content area were also highlighted (and retained). The result was a set of leadership standards that apply to literacy coaches without regard to the content area in which they are assisting teachers and a set of content area standards that apply to the demands that literacy coaches face when assisting in English language arts, math, science, or social studies.

Over the next several months the standards team members circulated the draft expectations among the leadership of the participating organizations and top reading researchers for further revision and comment. In February 2005 the organizations posted the working draft on their websites for public comment. Hundreds of reading experts, linguistic experts, literacy coaches, and content area teachers from around the country responded to the draft, providing valuable feedback on the contents of the standards and their clarity. Public comments were reviewed at a third standards meeting in June 2005, when the team developed a framework for revisions. Finally, a panel of practicing literacy coaches met at Carnegie Corporation to review the document and share their insights from the field.

In addition to the collective wisdom of educators, policymakers, reading and standards experts, many of the publications cited throughout this book guided the development of the *Standards for Middle and High School Literacy Coaches*. Kinsella's (2001) Reading Strategies Series, not otherwise cited, also provided important information on the particular demands of the reading and text structures in each of the four core content areas.

These standards are meant to complement IRA's *Standards for Reading Professionals— Revised 2003* (2004b), developed by reading professionals for reading professionals and thus silent on issues related to content area knowledge. Similarly, the content area organizations that are partners in this effort have standards for secondary teachers that do not focus on literacy specifically. The coaching standards address this chasm by including both literacy and content area knowledge and skills—particularly the specific reading and writing demands middle and high school students face in English language arts, mathematics, science, and social studies.

Part 3 of the standards comes out of the strong recommendation from the panel of coaches that the document be contextualized in the knowledge base of what is known about coaching and what some next steps might be. Catherine Snow, Jacy Ippolito, and Robert Schwartz examine the extant research literature to determine what we know and what we need to know about middle and high school literacy coaches. A working definition of a literacy coach is provided as well as a review of the specific challenges that face secondary coaches. The authors also suggest a research agenda that should be considered if literacy coaching is to be part of the fabric of U.S. middle and high schools.

Key Elements of Literacy Coaching

Standards for Middle and High School Literacy Coaches represents an ideal. Although accomplished literacy coaches may have many of the abilities and skills presented, few will meet all of the standards—at least initially. Coaches whose job it is to provide professional development will need rigorous professional development over the course of their employment, so they can sharpen the skills described in these standards (Russo, 2004). Experience indicates that while some expert teachers adapt quickly to the demands of literacy coaching, it takes two to three years for most to develop the full complement of coaching skills. Expanding this role to the middle and high school grades adds another dimension, as secondary coaches must assume the additional responsibility of working with colleagues across content areas. In hiring, employers may not be able to find individuals who meet all the standards. In those cases, the goal should be for literacy coaches to meet these standards over a reasonable period of time.

The coaching standards are organized into two parts—leadership standards and content area literacy standards. The leadership standards apply to literacy coaches without regard to the content area in which they are assisting teachers. The content area literacy standards apply to the demands literacy coaches face when assisting in a specific content area such as English language arts, mathematics, science, or social studies. Following is a summary of the four key competencies:

Leadership Standards

STANDARD 1: SKILLFUL COLLABORATORS
Content area literacy coaches are skilled collaborators who function effectively in middle school and/or high school settings.

STANDARD 2: SKILLFUL JOB-EMBEDDED COACHES
Content area literacy coaches are skilled instructional coaches for secondary teachers in the core content areas of English language arts, mathematics, science, and social studies.

STANDARD 3: SKILLFUL EVALUATORS OF LITERACY NEEDS
Content area literacy coaches are skilled evaluators of literacy needs within various subject areas and are able to collaborate with secondary school leadership teams and teachers to interpret and use assessment data to inform instruction.

Content Area Standard

STANDARD 4: SKILLFUL INSTRUCTIONAL STRATEGISTS
Content area literacy coaches are accomplished middle and high school teachers who are skilled in developing and implementing instructional strategies to improve academic literacy in the specific content area.

We expect several audiences will glean useful information from the standards, including

- **district administrators, school board members, and curriculum supervisors** as they develop job descriptions and identify criteria for hiring and assessing the success of coaches and the coaching program
- **school leaders**, including principals, department chairs, and other members of school leadership teams as they articulate shared goals and work to provide

coaches and teachers with the time and resources necessary for effective implementation of literacy coaching

- **parent groups and community stakeholders** as they help members of their organizations understand the role and importance of literacy coaches
- **university faculty** involved in teacher preparation programs as they develop and evaluate literacy coach preparation programs
- **accrediting agencies** (at both the state and federal levels) as they determine whether to accredit specific literacy coach preparation programs
- **literacy coaches** themselves as they set goals, establish benchmarks for their success, and evaluate their effectiveness

Conclusion

To compete and succeed in modern society, high school graduates need to be expert readers, writers, and communicators. Too many are not. Annually, hundreds of thousands of 12th graders on the threshold of graduating can barely read or write. Given the high stakes for these students and that we know a great deal about their literacy needs and the teaching practices that are effective with them, finding ways to put that knowledge immediately to work to improve the culture and conditions of secondary schools in the United States is an imperative. Equipping middle and high schools with trained literacy coaches is at least one line of attack to combat "the quiet resignation that seems to pervade education circles...that little if anything can be done" (Joftus, 2002, p. 1).

PART 1

Leadership Standards

The five organizations who have collaborated on these standards envision the role of secondary school literacy coaches as master teachers who provide essential leadership for the school's overall literacy program. A chief goal is to assist content area teachers in addressing the reading comprehension, writing, and communication skills that are particular to their disciplines. This includes activities that promote instructional reform, improve staff's capacity to use data, as well as actions directly aimed at supporting content area teachers at the building level with one-on-one demonstrations, observations, debriefings and classroom follow-ups, and small-group learning of new content and pedagogy. In a word, coaches are "embedded" within the daily action of schools.

If they are to succeed, according to Toll (2005), literacy coaches must be well versed in

- characteristics of adult learners
- processes for successful coaching
- essential elements of effective instruction
- literacy learning and processes
- measures of reading achievement

At the middle and high schools levels, in order to make informed recommendations, literacy coaches also must have sufficient knowledge of the specific content area in which they are assisting teachers. Although the standards include content-specific concepts in the four core areas, the expectation is not for literacy coaches to hold a degree in the content area or otherwise be an expert. They do, however, need to be adept enough to be able to assist with the literacy aspects of a lesson they are coaching. For example, while assisting a mathematics teacher, a literacy coach should be comfortable enough with the material being presented to assist the teacher in weaving literacy-based methods into the lesson in a manner that allows students to access the mathematics information, find their way through a written mathematics problem, and communicate their thinking in writing. Literacy coaches must understand the content of the lessons they are coaching. Teaching decoding, sight vocabulary, and spelling, among other basic skills, on the other hand, are not legitimate expectations of the secondary school literacy coach (or the content area teacher). Students who are performing far below grade level—young people who make it to middle and high school unable to read and comprehend even easy texts—need and deserve individual attention and intensive intervention in the fundamentals from tutors and other reading experts.

The expectation is that districts should hire individuals to be literacy coaches who hold a master's degree with an emphasis in literacy or reading or a reading certification endorsement. In addition to the necessary expertise in reading and literacy, secondary school literacy coaches who are highly regarded by content area teachers and understand the stresses and challenges of the secondary school culture hold the most promise. That's why many schools that have embraced literacy coaching seek experienced secondary teachers and then support them to gain the expertise they need in literacy to provide coaching to their school colleagues. Given the many demands of the role, the best candidates are those who are skilled listeners, good questioners, accomplished problem solvers, and professionals who embody strong reflective capabilities and are able to develop trusting relationships with a variety of people.

STANDARD 1: Skillful Collaborators

Content area literacy coaches are skilled collaborators who function effectively in middle school and/or high school settings.

ELEMENT 1.1 Working with the school's literacy team, literacy coaches determine the school's strengths (and need for improvement) in the area of literacy in order to improve students' reading, writing, and communication skills and content area achievement.

Performances

1.1.1 Literacy coaches assist the principal in developing a literacy team (if one does not already exist) composed of administrator(s), content teachers, resource teacher(s), and the literacy coach. Representatives of this team should be active on the school leadership team. If the school has a significant number of English-language learners (ELLs), then an English as a second language (ESL) teacher should be part of the team.

1.1.2 Literacy coaches collaborate with members of the literacy team and school leadership team to conduct a schoolwide literacy needs assessment.

1.1.3 Literacy coaches provide opportunities for small- and large-group discussions related to problems teachers are facing as a result of their students' poor literacy skills.

1.1.4 Literacy coaches communicate the findings of the school literacy needs assessment to staff and other stakeholders for their reflection and comment.

1.1.5 Using the needs assessment as a springboard for professional conversations, literacy coaches prioritize the needs and guide the development and implementation of a literacy improvement action plan that identifies

- specific, measurable literacy goals for each subject area

- specific literacy skills and strategies for each content area (and ESL classes) and other strategies common to all areas

- other activities and actions to support or extend schoolwide literacy learning

1.1.6 Literacy coaches help school staff align curriculum to state and district requirements, including identifying skill gaps between grades and providing continuous feedback from grade level to grade level.

1.1.7 Literacy coaches conduct ongoing evaluations of the literacy improvement action plan at the school. They

- review achievement data
- survey faculty, students, and parents on the effectiveness of literacy strategies that have been implemented at the school
- review data from class observations of teachers implementing literacy strategies and student engagement with them
- communicate results to staff and other stakeholders
- make plans for the continuation, modification, or addition of literacy strategies in response to the feedback data

1.1.8 Literacy coaches skillfully manage time and resources in support of literacy coaching.

Literacy Immersion Action Plan Closes Achievement Gap at Hopkins West Junior High

Hopkins West Junior High, located outside of Minneapolis, Minnesota, enjoyed a 90% pass rate on the Minnesota Minimum Basic Standards Test. The motivational spark for literacy immersion came, however, when school staff disaggregated the data to find a wide achievement gap existed for students of color and poverty. The leadership team plumbed the data and found poor reading and writing skills to be the source of the lower achievement. A literacy planning team quickly formed led by the seventh-grade teachers. The team narrowed the goals of the school improvement plan to two: literacy and equity. Subsequently, the school directed all fiscal and human resources toward developing a school culture that would support both. One of the first acts of the planning team was to revise the existing class schedule from 50-minute periods to an alternating-day block schedule that would extend instructional time to allow for the integration of literacy into daily content instruction. The new schedule also allowed a block of common planning time for teacher collaboration. The planning block permitted teachers to select appropriate literacy strategies, to model and refine lessons, as well as to evaluate student achievement and student work samples. The Hopkins school assessment team gathers each summer for a data retreat to strengthen its literacy focus and refine its action plan.

Source: Adapted from National Association of Secondary School Principals. (2005). *Creating a culture of literacy: A guide for middle and high school principals.* Reston, VA: Author.

ELEMENT 1.2 Literacy coaches promote productive relationships with and among school staff.

Performances

1.2.1 Literacy coaches showcase effective strategies employed by content area teachers and encourage teachers to share their stories of success with one another.

1.2.2 Literacy coaches listen to and learn about the needs and concerns of students, staff, and parents and respond in a manner that inspires trust, communicates respect, and is nonjudgmental in nature.

1.2.3 Literacy coaches understand and respect issues of confidentiality.

1.2.4 Literacy coaches know what it means to be a coach and how that differs from being a supervisor.

1.2.5 Literacy coaches respond promptly to requests for assistance from teachers and school leaders.

1.2.6 Literacy coaches facilitate discussions between and among the leadership team and teachers on issues related to adolescent literacy. They set meeting agendas based on staff input and their own assessment of what students in various grade levels and content areas need to work on to meet district or school goals as outlined in the school's literacy improvement action plan.

1.2.7 Literacy coaches understand the secondary school culture and student, as well as the stresses and dilemmas secondary content area teachers must confront.

1.2.8 Literacy coaches demonstrate positive expectations for students' learning and share that vision of students' potential with teachers. This includes understanding the second-language acquisition process ELLs go through and conveying this to the teachers.

1.2.9 Literacy coaches apply concepts of adult learning and motivation in order to meet the needs of school staff who are in various stages of their careers. This includes using varied group configurations and presentation formats as needed to engage adult learners and identifying appropriate professional development settings and schedules.

1.2.10 Literacy coaches encourage language specialists in the school (e.g., ESL and reading teachers) to serve as resources for content area teachers to learn more about how students, especially ELLs, learn language.

1.2.11 Literacy coaches work to keep administrators informed and involved and enlist administrators' support for teachers with their literacy efforts.

Equipping Teachers With Core Repertoire of Literacy Strategies Spells Success for J.E.B. Stuart High School

J.E.B. Stuart High School, located outside of Washington, D.C., is beating the statistical odds. With a student body that is 66% second-language learners and more than 50% below the poverty line, the school moved from the bottom levels of achievement to the peak of academic success by addressing students' poor attendance and weak reading skills. Eight years ago, 76% of students were reading below grade level; today, only a handful of students are behind. Initially the teaching staff was openly hostile to instituting a literacy program. Staff worried they would be unable to cover course content and teach literacy strategies too. Teachers also felt ill-equipped to teach reading strategies to students. Student achievement data was key to convincing staff they needed to make a dramatic change if they were to meet the learning needs of their students. A professional development program designed to provide teachers with a core repertoire of 15 literacy immersion strategies at the secondary level, followed up with peer teaching and observations, gave content teachers the confidence they needed to include those strategies in their daily instruction.

Source: Adapted from National Association of Secondary School Principals. (2005). *Creating a culture of literacy: A guide for middle and high school principals.* Reston, VA: Author.

ELEMENT 1.3 Literacy coaches strengthen their professional teaching knowledge, skills, and strategies.

Performances

1.3.1 Literacy coaches stay current with professional literature and the latest research on promising practices for adolescent literacy and adolescent ELL language development.

1.3.2 Literacy coaches routinely examine best practices and curriculum materials related to adolescent literacy for native and nonnative speakers of English.

1.3.3 Literacy coaches act in a manner that demonstrates their openness to new ideas.

1.3.4 Literacy coaches meet regularly (at least monthly) with other coaches in the school or school district to build professional skills and a sense of community.

1.3.5 Literacy coaches attend professional seminars, conventions, and other training in order to receive instruction on a core set of research-based literacy strategies and strategies for working with ELLs (both those literate and not literate in their native language) as well as to learn how to work effectively with adult learners.

Coaching for the Coaches

Every Friday in the Campbell Union District, San Jose, California, the coaches meet together with the Director of Curriculum and Professional Development for half- or full-day professional development sessions. The district requires each coach to keep track of his or her monthly workshops and daily sessions with individual teachers. They record what's working, concerns and challenges, and next steps in Collaborative Journals. Coaches use their weekly time together to share strategies, discuss challenges, and hone upcoming presentations. At the end of the year, they present their work to the Campbell school board. Annually, the district surveys teachers on how often they use a specific checklist of literacy strategies and the extent to which those strategies were effective. Accountability also takes the form of principal feedback on whether they see evidence of literacy strategies on which the teachers have been coached.

Source: Adapted from Symonds, K.W. (2003). *Literacy coaching: How school districts can support a long-term strategy in a short-term world.* Oakland, CA: Bay Area School Reform Collaborative.

STANDARD 2: Skillful Job-Embedded Coaches

Content area literacy coaches are skilled instructional coaches for secondary teachers in the core content areas of English language arts, mathematics, science, and social studies.

ELEMENT 2.1 Literacy coaches work with teachers individually, in collaborative teams, and/or with departments, providing practical support on a full range of reading, writing, and communication strategies.

Performances

2.1.1 Literacy coaches assist teachers in the analysis and selection of diverse content area texts and instructional materials that link to multiple ability levels and multicultural perspectives, and connect to students' backgrounds, interests, and English language proficiency levels.

2.1.2 Literacy coaches assist teachers in developing instruction designed to improve students' abilities to read and understand content area texts and to spur student interest in more complex reading materials. They

- plan instruction around what teachers want students to learn from the text
- identify what might make it hard for students to learn from the text
- identify how teachers might use classroom time differently in order to improve reading for understanding
- select strategies to help teachers meet content goals and student needs
- determine what a teacher can do if students "don't get it" the first time
- identify appropriate literacy scaffolding strategies that accommodate ELLs' different proficiency levels but move them toward grade-level literacy

2.1.3 Literacy coaches provide content area teachers with professional development related to metacognitive reading strategies such as

- before-reading strategies: set purpose (information or pleasure), make distinct connections to prior knowledge, identify key terms, assess level of difficulty/ length of selection, understand text organization and use text clues (headings, captions, photos, graphics, first/last paragraphs, key words such as sequence terms), and gain general sense of the topic/subtopics
- during-reading strategies: look for key concepts/main ideas and relate each paragraph to those, think out loud and ask questions of the text, apply various vocabulary techniques to understand unfamiliar words, take notes, and backtrack when confused
- after-reading strategies: confirm key concepts/main ideas, review reading, create graphic organizers, form opinions, write a summary, and synthesize information from several sources

2.1.4 Literacy coaches provide professional development related to literacy strategies that content area teachers could adopt and adapt for use in their classrooms, such as

- teacher modeling (involves teachers reading aloud texts and making their strategies and practices readily apparent to students)
- scaffolded instruction (involves teachers giving high support for students practicing new skills and then slowly decreasing that support to increase student self-sufficiency; also includes using oral language skills as a springboard to reading and writing skills for ELLs)
- apprenticeship models (involves teachers engaging students in content-centered learning partnerships)

2.1.5 Literacy coaches explore with content area teachers crosscultural communication patterns in speaking and writing and their relationship with literacy skills in English.

2.1.6 Literacy coaches have a repertoire of reading strategies at their disposal to share with and model for content area teachers (e.g., reciprocal teaching [Palincsar & Brown, 1984], K-W-L [Ogle, 1986], Directed Reading and Thinking Activity [Stauffer, 1969]). Literacy coaches help teachers determine which of these strategies are best used with the content being taught.

2.1.7 Literacy coaches provide professional development related to multiple vocabulary development strategies and help teachers determine which of these strategies are best used with the content being taught. Examples include

- contextual approaches (surrounding words and sentences; definitions in text through restatement, examples, and comparison and contrast)
- morphological approaches (study of the structure of words)
- cognates (words that have the same root or origin)
- definitional approaches (using related words to find meanings of unknown words such as *ideal/idealism, fallacy/fallacious*)
- signal words (words that alert reader that new information or certain information is coming)

2.1.8 Literacy coaches assist teachers with increasing the amount of writing instruction students receive and the amount of writing they do, as well as the quality and appropriateness of writing instruction and assignments. They also assist teachers with scaffolding writing genres particular to different content areas (e.g., lab reports, geometric proofs).

2.1.9 Literacy coaches provide professional development related to strategies to help students analyze and evaluate Internet sources for their usefulness, credibility, reliability, and consistency. This includes evaluating Internet sources written in a native language of some students.

2.1.10 Literacy coaches link teachers to evidence-based current research to help make research more tangible and applicable to their classrooms.

Literacy Coaches Link Content Teachers to Current Research

In East Side Union High School District (CA), literacy coaches make sure that teachers get access to the latest information. "Teachers don't have time to go on the Net and research," said Literacy Coach Muscio. Her colleague has created a strategy binder for each teacher called "A Good Reader Binder," which culls information from various sources on teaching reading and provides tools such as question trees and anticipation guides. Another coach writes a monthly publication titled "Literacy Tips" that contains strategies teachers can use across the curriculum. In one tip titled "What to do when there is time left at the end of the period," the coach suggested different ways to guide students to reflect on what they've learned, including an Exit Ticket and a 3x5 card for responses to questions like, "What remains confusing to me at this point is..." and "What I know now that I did not know before is...."

Source: Adapted from Symonds, K.W. (2003). *Literacy coaching: How school districts can support a long-term strategy in a short-term world.* Oakland, CA: Bay Area School Reform Collaborative.

ELEMENT 2.2 Literacy coaches observe and provide feedback to teachers on instruction related to literacy development and content area knowledge.

Performances

2.2.1 Literacy coaches help to ensure that teachers understand that observations are not a threatening device but rather a tool to spark discussion and to reinforce the literacy emphasis within the school.

2.2.2 Literacy coaches regularly conduct observations of content classes to collect informal data on teacher use of instructional strategies and student engagement with the strategies aimed at increasing teachers' knowledge and skill at delivering literacy instruction.

2.2.3 Before and after observations, literacy coaches engage in reflective dialogue with teachers to

- clarify lesson objectives, including teachers' personal goals in delivering the lesson
- determine how to assess what students have learned
- identify the successes and challenges encountered in the lesson and what could be improved in terms of lesson content and delivery
- focus on next steps, including how teachers might adjust instruction and instructional settings to meet a range of literacy needs of individual students, including ELLs, and to foster learning in the content area

2.2.4 Literacy coaches demonstrate instructional strategies and provide ongoing support to teachers as they try out the strategies themselves.

Productive Observations, Productive Relationships

In Campbell Union District in California, observations are used frequently in the coaching cycle, with a conference before and after each classroom visit to ensure that teachers feel supported and receive constructive feedback to improve their practice. As Coach Kathleen McCowan reflects, "If you've just done a lesson, I'll say, 'Well, how do you think it went?' If the teacher then replies, 'Boy, I sure fell down there!' then we can work on that together. I'm not going to say, 'That was terrible'...that would fall under evaluation." If the lesson is weak, however, she finds a way to raise the important issues. The goal is to have teachers leave the post-conference with a sense of accomplishment and a plan of action for what they will do next in their own classrooms.

Source: Adapted from Symonds, K.W. (2003). *Literacy coaching: How school districts can support a long-term strategy in a short-term world.* Oakland, CA: Bay Area School Reform Collaborative.

STANDARD 3: Skillful Evaluators of Literacy Needs

Content area literacy coaches are skilled evaluators of literacy needs within various subject areas and are able to collaborate with secondary school leadership teams and teachers to interpret and use assessment data to inform instruction.

ELEMENT 3.1 Literacy coaches lead faculty in the selection and use of a range of assessment tools as a means to make sound decisions about student literacy needs as related to the curriculum and to instruction.

Performances

3.1.1 Literacy coaches develop a comprehensive assessment program that uses both formal and informal measures of achievement, including the use of

- content area standardized assessments in order to evaluate individual and school achievement and to track group progress from year to year
- specific literacy pre- and post-tests
- assessments that measure students' native language literacy skills
- English language development assessments for ELLs
- content area reading inventories that determine students' abilities to use text features and match reading abilities of students to level of text readability
- authentic assessments that test students' abilities to read a particular text in a content area and then write about it
- informal assessments such as teacher anecdotal records, student reflective journals, student strategy-use records, and/or student surveys
- student surveys about adolescent literacy practices outside of the classroom and topics of interest for reading and writing (in English and/or another language)

3.1.2 Literacy coaches set schedules for administering and analyzing formative and summative assessments in order to ensure assessments are able to inform instruction and become a tool for improvement.

3.1.3 As teachers implement new instructional literacy strategies, literacy coaches aid in the design and/or implementation of formative assessments to determine whether the strategy was successful.

3.1.4 Literacy coaches help teachers to standardize the scoring of writing and other measures of literacy.

3.1.5 Literacy coaches know current research and trends in assessment methodologies.

Student Assessment Data in the Driver's Seat at Stuart High School

To determine the literacy skills of its students, J.E.B. Stuart High School (Fairfax County, VA) insists on administering the Gates-McGinnity to all eighth graders who are scheduled to enter their school. The school selected this assessment tool because it was normed on a student population that reflected its own, i.e., English-language learners and students in poverty. Incoming freshmen who score below the 40th percentiles take a follow-up individual reading inventory to diagnose specific reading problems. This data directs the development of a plan to address targeted reading deficits. The literacy coach works with content area teachers to tailor instruction to the reading levels of various students as well as model specific strategies to help students better comprehend content texts, such as history and science textbooks.

Source: Adapted from National Association of Secondary School Principals. (2005). *Creating a culture of literacy: A guide for middle and high school principals.* Reston, VA: Author.

ELEMENT 3.2 As dynamic supports for reflection and action, literacy coaches conduct regular meetings with content area teachers to examine student work and monitor progress.

Performances

3.2.1 Literacy coaches introduce content area teachers to ways to observe adolescents' literacy skills and ELLs' language development progress, and to derive meaning from those observations.

3.2.2 Literacy coaches host periodic meetings (held monthly or at the end of each grading period) with content area teachers during which they examine student work and evaluate their success with literacy strategies in light of formative and, when available, summative assessment data.

3.2.3 Literacy coaches help teachers analyze trends on content area achievement tests, including identifying

- whether student scores are consistently low and/or high in particular skill areas
- the progress of specific grade levels or departmental teams
- the achievement of different groups of students (e.g., data disaggregated by race or socioeconomic level)
- the growth of ELL progress toward English language proficiency

3.2.4 Literacy coaches help teachers use the analysis of various assessment results to determine which strategies—content or literacy—will move students to higher levels of achievement.

Time and Focus on Literacy Produce Stunning Turnaround for Vocational School in California

Duncan Polytechnical High School in Fresno shed its 1980s designation as an occupational training school for dropouts to become one of California's highest achieving schools: Currently, 82% of its 10th graders pass the California tests for mathematics and reading/language arts. Literacy immersion is at the heart of the school's stunning transition. Teachers at Duncan recognized that students' abilities to read and write well were key to understanding technical manuals and preparing for rewarding vocational careers. In addition to intensive summer training at area colleges, a lead literacy teacher was selected to model and talk over effective literacy strategies with content teachers during daily 30-minute professional development blocks that the school secured for teachers by expanding their lunch hours. In the first years of the new literacy focus, teachers learned strategies to support effective use of textbooks in their content areas. In addition, Silent Sustained Reading was instituted as a daily 20-minute activity. During this period, students read self-selected books and their teachers read right along with them—no other activities allowed. In subsequent years, the literacy program was expanded to focus on new ideas and strategies to fully integrate writing across the curriculum. Every summer, teachers and administrators carefully analyze student data and student work in order to plan the next year's professional development to support (and sustain high levels of) student achievement.

Source: Adapted from National Association of Secondary School Principals. (2005). *Creating a culture of literacy: A guide for middle and high school principals.* Reston, VA: Author.

PART 2

Content Area Literacy Standards

English Language Arts

The vision guiding IRA and NCTE's (1996) *Standards for the English Language Arts* is that all students must be offered "the opportunities, the encouragement, and the vision to develop the language skills they need to pursue life's goals, including personal enrichment and participation as informed members of our society" (p. 1). Due to the close connection between language skills and literacy development, English teachers are often called on to bear the bulk, if not the entirety, of the responsibility for students' literacy—this despite the fact that they, similar to colleagues from other disciplines, do not typically benefit from extensive preparation in teaching secondary students who are poor readers and writers. Thus the opportunity to work in partnership with literacy coaches who can facilitate schoolwide approaches to advancing literacy skills is extremely valuable to our members.

Data show that 25% of high school students are not able to identify the main idea of a passage; many tend to dwell on details and subordinate ideas (Kamil, 2003). Research reveals that comprehension failure is attributed to the text processing skills of these readers who, among other things, are often unaware of the purpose for reading and thus are less apt to modify their reading rates (Smith, 1967); less able to detect text inconsistencies, the logical structure of text, or how ideas are interconnected (DiVesta, Hayward, & Orlando 1979; Owings, Peterson, Bransford, Morris, & Stein, 1980); and less sensitive to semantic and syntactic cues in text (Irakson & Miller, 1978). Generally speaking, poor readers are not as flexible as skilled readers in adapting their reading processes to the demands of the task or capitalizing on the structure inherent in texts. Consequently, their ability to write clearly or understand complex subject matter across the content areas is inhibited.

Inexperienced adolescent readers need opportunities and instructional support to read many and diverse types of texts in order to gain experience, build fluency, and develop a range as readers. Through extensive reading of a range of texts, supported by strategy lessons and discussions, readers become familiar with written language structures and text features, develop their vocabularies, and read for meaning more efficiently and effectively. Conversations about their reading that focus on the strategies they use and their language knowledge help adolescents build confidence in their reading and become better readers. Middle and high school English classes are an excellent place to move students to deeper understandings of texts and increase their ability to generate ideas and knowledge for their own uses and to meet scholastic challenges across the curriculum.

The literacy coach can play an essential role in assisting English teachers as they strive to

- bridge between adolescents' rich literate backgrounds and school literacy
- work on schoolwide teams to teach literacy in each discipline as an essential way of learning in the disciplines
- recognize when students are not making meaning with text and provide appropriate, strategic assistance to read course content effectively
- facilitate student-initiated conversations regarding texts that are authentic and relevant to real life experiences
- create environments that allow students to engage in critical examinations of texts as they dissect, deconstruct, and reconstruct in an effort to engage in meaning making and comprehension processes

STANDARD 4: Skillful Instructional Strategists

Content area literacy coaches are accomplished middle and high school teachers who are skilled in developing and implementing instructional strategies to improve academic literacy in English language arts.

ELEMENT 4.1 Literacy coaches are familiar with the English language arts content area and know how reading and writing processes intersect with the discipline of English language arts.

Performances

4.1.1 Literacy coaches know and understand the IRA and NCTE professional standards and benchmarks as well as those of the Teachers of English to Speakers of Other Languages (see www.tesol.org/s_tesol/seccss.asp?CID=86&DID=1556) and how they relate to state and local student standards in English language arts and to ELL development.

4.1.2 Literacy coaches relate adolescent development and students' linguistic and cultural backgrounds to the study of English language arts content, skills, and dispositions in a manner that helps English language arts teachers bridge young adult contemporary and classic literature. They help teachers identify cultural biases and embedded sociocultural knowledge in text as well as ways to implement strategies to build background for ELLs concerning the topics of the text.

4.1.3 Literacy coaches know the specific demands of reading English language arts textbooks and other literary texts, including

- distinguishing informational text from narrative text in order to guide students to use the right strategies
- distinguishing fact from opinion and the words that signal opinions and judgments in persuasive essays
- the technical nature of the vocabulary demands that require preteaching (e.g., new literary terms, conceptual vocabulary, multiple-meaning words)

- thinking critically (e.g., drawing inferences or conclusions from text, analyzing author's purpose and point of view, evaluating author's argument and evidence, synthesizing information from more than one text)
- how to use visual aids such as charts and diagrams that clarify the particular lesson
- how to use other aids such as glossaries and appendixes that pertain to reading, writing, and English language conventions

4.1.4 Literacy coaches help teachers select multicultural texts that connect with students' interests and backgrounds and with state and local standards.

ELEMENT 4.2 Literacy coaches demonstrate multiple comprehension strategies to assist content area teachers in developing active and competent readers within the English language arts.

Performances

4.2.1 Literacy coaches know and assist English language arts teachers in understanding the text structures that students commonly encounter in literary text selections, including

- narrative text structure (e.g., asking students to retell or summarize stories, including important details pertaining to their events, setting, theme, and what the characters say and do; asking students to infer motives of characters and the causal relations among events)
- description or main idea and detail text structure (e.g., asking students to look for the topic, the main points, and supporting details, making notes in a wheel-and-spoke diagram)
- comparison and contrast text structure (e.g., looking for signal words; asking students to record differences and similarities between people, places, or events in a Venn diagram)
- chronological/sequential text structure (e.g., looking for signal words; asking students to create a sequence chart of events)
- cause and effect text structure (e.g., looking for signal words; asking students to make predictions and determine relationships between events and the way characters behave)
- argument and evidence text structure (e.g., asking students to list the argument and the evidence to help them make their own judgments)
- combination of patterns (e.g., asking students to find several text structures in a language arts selection)

4.2.2 Literacy coaches assist English language arts teachers in matching instructional methods to the dominant pattern of text structure for any given reading (e.g., developing a timeline for a reading that is organized chronologically or completing a Venn diagram for a reading that is organized in a comparison/contrast pattern).

4.2.3 Literacy coaches know and model methods and strategies to assist English language arts teachers to engage students actively in learning, including asking students to express and defend the point of view of authors as well as develop and express an informed point of view of their own. Some examples of active learning strategies that promote student discussion and dialogue include role plays, think–pair–share, jigsaw, pair problem solving, fishbowl, and round robin strategies.

4.2.4 Literacy coaches know and model strategies for supporting students with the writing process and the characteristics of different types of expository and imaginative writing.

Literacy Strategies Deepen Students' Thinking in English Language Arts Class

Before becoming a literacy coach in Boston, Chloe had taught English for 10 years at both the college and high school levels. In her work with a young English teacher at a Boston high school, Chloe was able to help the teacher develop ongoing book clubs and use reading strategies that connected one reading to another in order to deepen students' thinking. The coach counted it as a real success when she observed students discussing the text and offering their ideas—with the teacher at the side, not at the center of the room directing the conversation. Another English teacher sought suggestions for ways to help students understand that there can be more than one interpretation of a text as long as it can be substantiated. Chloe suggested working with the Roethke poem "My Papa's Waltz" because it was short and accessible to students, and could be handled in one day. She and the teacher talked over how the poem could be interpreted as a nostalgic reverie about childhood or a lens on childhood abuse. Using a protocol adapted from Sheridan Blau's *The Literature Workshop*, the coach helped to design an activity that asked students to:

1. Underline words or lines they found confusing, then write out questions.

2. Choose the most important line in the poem and write a paragraph about why.

3. Get together in groups of four to share problems they had with specific words and lines and work to clear them up.

4. Then share their paragraphs about the most important line they picked and discuss the similarities and differences in their perspectives.

Source: Adapted from Annenberg Institute for School Reform. (2005). *Coaches in the high school classroom: Studies in implementing high school reform* (Prepared for Carnegie Corporation of New York). Providence, RI: Author.

Mathematics

Much of our world can be modeled and understood through mathematics. Those who understand and can use mathematics will have opportunities that others do not. Mathematics educators are dedicated to translating mathematical knowledge, positive attitudes, and high expectations to students of diverse backgrounds and strengths so that all are actively engaged and learning at high levels. NCTM's (2000) *Principles and Standards for School Mathematics* describes "a future in which all students have access to rigorous, high-quality mathematics instruction."

Much of the study of mathematics is an experience in reasoning and problem solving. Beyond acquiring procedural mathematical skills with their clear methods and boundaries, students need to master the higher order skills of reading, interpreting, and representing life situations in mathematical settings. Communication skills are integral to mathematics literacy and numeracy. Students gain insights when they are asked to present their methods, justify their reasoning to a classmate or teacher, or formulate a question about something that is puzzling to them. Written and oral communication prompt reflection, refinement, discussion, and amendment. They help students to consolidate their thinking and clarify their thoughts about the ideas developed in the lesson. Listening to the explanations of others gives students opportunities to further their own understandings. Despite the utility of talking and writing, students do not necessarily talk or write about mathematics naturally, especially as it becomes more complex and abstract.

Many mathematical textbooks are marked by particular characteristics such as a density of concepts that require slower reading than narrative texts, concepts that build from chapter to chapter, common words that have different meanings in mathematics, and equations and symbols that communicate certain meanings. Visual literacy abilities also are essential. Key mathematical information is represented in a variety of forms. Diagrams, tables, charts, and graphs can serve as vehicles for presenting key mathematical concepts with the accompanying text acting as an explanation. Supports for students and their teachers are vital here, such as that provided by literacy coaches.

Providing students with the ability to attack and solve problems in a wide variety of settings is a principal goal of mathematics education. Problem solving means engaging in a task for which the solution method is not known in advance, and in order to find an answer, students must draw from their prior knowledge and exercise their computational, procedural, and reasoning skills. To become able problem solvers, students need extensive opportunities to formulate questions and grapple with, model, and solve engaging problems at various levels of difficulty. Students need to be able to test ideas, try different approaches, explain their reasoning, check their results for errors and reasonableness, and devise independent ways to verify results. Through problem solving, students acquire ways of thinking, habits of persistence and curiosity, and confidence to confront unfamiliar situations—good practice for what they will face outside the mathematics classroom. Choosing problems wisely and using and adapting problems from instructional materials pose a difficult challenge for many teachers. This is another area in which literary coaches can be invaluable: Appropriate analysis of the demands of a problem, the mathematical ideas that are addressed, and likely student questions help to assure teachers that the selected problems will further student learning and the mathematical goals for the class.

We are convinced that a supportive relationship between the literacy coach and the classroom teacher can serve as a catalyst for rich conversations and can serve to improve the teaching techniques and strategies of subject area teachers. Moreover, the stronger the literacy coach's background in mathematics, the more able he or she will be to provide content teachers with skills and knowledge to enhance student learning.

STANDARD 4: Skillful Instructional Strategists

Content area literacy coaches are accomplished middle and high school teachers who are skilled in developing and implementing instructional strategies to improve academic literacy in mathematics.

ELEMENT 4.1 Literacy coaches are familiar with the mathematics content area and know how reading and writing processes intersect with the disciplines included in mathematics.

Performances

4.1.1 Literacy coaches know and understand the NCTM content and process standards and how they relate to state and local student standards in mathematics.

4.1.2 Literacy coaches relate adolescent development and students' linguistic and cultural backgrounds to the study of mathematics content, skills, and dispositions.

4.1.3 Literacy coaches know the specific demands of reading mathematics textbooks and relating mathematical words to the physical world, including

- the density of ideas (e.g., requiring slower reading rates than for narrative texts; asking students to stop when they do not understand an idea, express the idea in their words, and seek an alternate explanation when necessary)

- concepts that build within a chapter or across chapters (e.g., asking students to back track to see if comprehension problems stem from lack of understanding of previously learned concepts)

- the technical nature of the vocabulary demands and the mathematical meaning of multiple-meaning words (e.g., *factor, plane, table, function*)

- the use of equations and symbols to model life situations (e.g., asking students to create or restate in words or sentences the relation between the symbols and the situation being modeled)

- text with diagrams and graphs (e.g., asking students to interpret the diagram or graph while they read the explanation)

- using the power of different representations (e.g., words, tables, graphs, hands-on objects, and equations) to aid students in understanding the underlying mathematical concept, matching each representation to the learning styles of different individuals

- the possibility that some students from other countries are used to different symbols or procedures to read and solve equations or problems (e.g., use of a comma rather than a decimal)

ELEMENT 4.2 Literacy coaches know and understand multiple comprehension strategies to assist content area teachers in developing active and competent readers within the discipline of mathematics.

Performances

4.2.1 Literacy coaches know and assist mathematics teachers in understanding the text structures that students commonly encounter in mathematics, including

- description or main idea and detail text structure (e.g., asking students to identify the topic, the main points, and supporting details)
- definition text structure (e.g., asking students what is being defined and to locate the definition)

4.2.2 Literacy coaches assist mathematics teachers in assessing the literacy demands of applied mathematics problems that are usually presented in oral or written formats, including multiple-meaning vocabulary words and the sometimes complicated syntax.

4.2.3 Literacy coaches know and model the way logic and reasoning are used in mathematical contexts such as

- making and testing the validity of conjectures
- reasoning inductively from patterns and specific cases
- making deductive arguments using mathematical truths established in class
- developing and evaluating informal proof by contradiction
- understanding and producing mathematical proofs (logically rigorous deductions of conclusions from hypotheses)

4.2.4 Literacy coaches know and model methods and strategies to assist mathematics teachers to engage students actively in learning and problem solving through dialogue, discussions, and group projects (e.g., think–pair–share, jigsaw, pair problem solving, fishbowl, and round robin strategies).

4.2.5 Literacy coaches know and model strategies for representing mathematical ideas in a variety of modes (e.g., literal, symbolic, graphic), which includes asking students to restate symbolic representations (e.g., numerals, equations, graphs) in words or sentences.

Two Brothers Lead the Charge for Literacy Skills at Mundelein High School

When Dan Szymkowiak and his brother, Dennis, got together for a family gathering, conversation invariably turned to the increasing challenge they were facing trying to teach students in their classes who had inadequate reading skills. Veteran teachers at Mundelein High School located in a suburb north of Chicago, they—one a mathematics teacher and the other an English teacher—decided it was time to make a full court press to address students' literacy skills as a means of securing their students' grasp of course content. Working from existing research, the two found ways to make literacy a foundation of their respective classes: They adopted a common language and some common strategies for helping kids process the content.

These days, Dan asks students in his mathematics classes what they know about a topic before they start reading in their textbook. Together with his students, he reviews new or difficult vocabulary words. He instructs his students how to take notes and to summarize regularly as they read to ensure they really understand what they are reading. He also asks students to explain their thoughts and challenges as they solve problems. In brother Dennis's ninth-grade English class, students are encouraged to anticipate the topics they might encounter as they read. For example, after reviewing the graphics and reading the title, headlines, and first and last paragraphs for a particular article in a magazine, students make predictions about what the piece is likely about and the kind of information it is likely to contain. After students read the piece thoroughly, they check to see if their predictions are accurate.

For the Szymkowiak brothers, convincing their colleagues that literacy is a critical part of their jobs has not been easy. But the efforts have paid off. "We can see from some of our data that certain individuals who combine traditional instruction with literacy strategies, their students are doing better," says Dennis Szymkowiak. "Building reading skills doesn't cut into teaching literature, math, or science.... It's part of it."

Source: Adapted from Manzo, K.K. (2005, February 16). Dynamic duo. *Education Week, 24*(23), pp. 37–39.

Science

NSTA's mission is to promote excellence and innovation in science teaching and learning for all. The vision presented in the *National Science Education Standards* (National Research Council, 1996) recognizes how integral literacy is to the study of the sciences:

> Inquiry is a multifaceted activity that involves making observations; posing questions; examining books and other sources of information to see what is already known; planning investigations; reviewing what is known in light of experimental evidence; using tools to gather, analyze, and interpret data; proposing answers, explanations, and predictions, and communicating the results.

Although many young people can make predictions about scientific phenomena and can even carry out rudimentary investigations, state and national testing data demonstrate that few students can produce explanations of their findings in ways that build on the discursive practices of science (e.g., supporting claims with evidence, explaining one's reasoning). These data do not directly equate with the learning capacity students possess or to the instructional experiences and support they receive. They link, in good part, to students' literacy skills—the ability to use reading, writing, and communication skills effectively—both in learning new ideas and in communicating understanding of those ideas in science classrooms.

In *The New Science Literacy*, Their and Daviss (2002) detail the specific reading, writing, and oral communication demands that students encounter in science classes. They note how scientific reading is concept-laden and how one concept often builds on another, so students cannot skip over a concept and expect to understand or catch up later. Diagrams, concept-laden vocabulary, abbreviations, equations, and processes also pose challenges. Moreover, it is not unusual for students to find an array of articles and studies on a scientific issue with conflicting messages. To interpret the materials' collective meanings, students must learn how to evaluate the information and presentation strategies of the various selections. Students also need to understand how to analyze different kinds of evidence and their relative weight and importance.

Special forms of writing in science also require special instruction. In most science classes, students are expected to write narratives of the step-by-step procedures they conduct in their investigations. The object of such a report is not only to explain what students did but also to explain their procedures well enough so others can replicate the instructions and reach the same result. Good science is synonymous with the precise use of language.

In addition to reading and writing, the importance of oral communication skills cannot be overestimated. In science classrooms, students often work in groups, demanding special skills beyond everyday or casual conversation. Students sort through and hone their ideas by talking about them and finding out how other people think and react to issues. Such group interaction requires instant analysis, comprehension, judgment, and response—skills that require careful focus and instruction.

Unfortunately, few science teachers are required to take more than one literacy methods course during teacher preparation programs, yet it is fundamental that teachers know how to

- assess the appropriateness of texts to use with students in teaching

- assess the literacy demands of a given science lesson and how to help all students

- access content from textbooks, the Internet, and other science materials

- assist students with the research process and how to share findings in scientifically appropriate ways and

- work with struggling or second-language learners for whom science language and discourse may produce additional reading and writing challenges

When professional development taps into the challenges teachers face every day and provides opportunities for learning new strategies and the collegial support to make changes—which is the goal of these literacy standards—science educators will have the opportunity to reflect on our teaching, explore solutions, and redirect our actions based on new information.

STANDARD 4: Skillful Instructional Strategists

Content area literacy coaches are accomplished middle and high school teachers who are skilled in using their knowledge of in-depth science learning to support the implementation of instructional strategies that improve academic literacy in science.

ELEMENT 4.1 Literacy coaches have understanding of the instructional goals of the science subject matter area and are knowledgeable about how the processes of reading and writing are used within the discipline of science.

Performances

4.1.1 Literacy coaches know and understand the *National Science Education Standards* (National Research Council, 1996) and *Benchmarks for Science Literacy* (American Association for Advancement of Science, 1993) and how they relate to state and local standards.

4.1.2 Literacy coaches have in-depth understanding of the science content, skills, and dispositions to be learned by students. In particular, literacy coaches understand how effective science instruction can impact or challenge adolescent preconceptions of scientific understandings and dispositions.

4.1.3 Literacy coaches know the specific demands of reading science textbooks with comprehension, including

- how to relate what is read to relevant prior knowledge

- density of ideas requires students to stop when they do not understand ideas (and seek additional explanations)

- concepts that build within and across chapters require students to relate what is read to relevant prior knowledge (based on student understanding of previously learned concepts)

- the technical nature of science requires continuing review of what has been previously learned
- distinguishing between facts based on empirical/scientific findings from opinion
- ability to use scientific knowledge to draw inferences or conclusions from facts, discern cause and effect relationships, detect fallacies in authors' evidence, and support own claims with evidence
- following instructions to perform laboratory activities step by step in a disciplined fashion
- explaining diagrams and graphs in text in terms of scientific content/meaning
- explaining meaning of abbreviations and symbols (e.g., asking students to put abbreviations, symbols, and equations into words)

ELEMENT 4.2 **Literacy coaches are able to assist science area teachers to use investigation, reading comprehension, writing, speaking, and listening strategies to help students become active and competent learners of science.**

Performances

4.2.1 Literacy coaches are able to work collaboratively with science teachers to implement model strategies in science classrooms that enhance student understanding of science text materials, including

- identifying core science concepts and concept relationships presented in text; developing propositional concept maps to organize concepts/relationships and to illustrate concepts/relationships with examples
- identifying hierarchical concept relationships in science and the associated characteristics that determine levels of classification
- identifying cause–effect relationships within a domain of science and using such knowledge to make predictions and explain multiple experiments that illustrate their meaning
- requiring students to sequence scientific information or events in "real-time" temporal, causal, or a history-of-science order
- asking students to use scientific knowledge to analyze various hypotheses, arguments, points of view, and perspectives about scientific issues

4.2.2 Literacy coaches are able to work collaboratively with science teachers to implement model strategies in science classrooms that use logic and reasoning in scientific contexts such as

- using methods of science for making and testing the validity of hypotheses or conjectures
- reasoning inductively from science facts
- making deductive arguments using scientific knowledge learned in class
- establishing the boundaries and conditions of established knowledge
- systematically discrediting, destroying, or supporting propositions, as appropriate, through the use of precise and relevant evidence

4.2.3 Literacy coaches are able to work collaboratively with science teachers to implement model strategies in science classrooms that teach students to write clear and testable questions; design and describe laboratory procedures; record observations; and use evidence and logical thinking to develop, write, and defend their explanations.

4.2.4 Literacy coaches are able to work collaboratively with science teachers to implement model strategies in science classrooms that engage students in learning through discourse, discussions, and group projects (e.g., think–pair–share, jigsaw, pair problem solving, fishbowl, and round robin strategies).

4.2.5 Literacy coaches are able to work collaboratively with science teachers to implement model strategies in science classrooms that use knowledge-based procedures for representing scientific concepts and concept relationships in textual, symbolic, and graphics modes.

4.2.6 Literacy coaches are able to work collaboratively with science teachers to implement model strategies in science classrooms that teach students how to write and/or deliver oral presentations to a wide variety of audiences that use scientific knowledge to explain, argue, or defend scientific conclusions, theories, and ideas.

With Attention to Literacy, Chemistry Students in Oakland High School Jump Ahead

When Willard Brown, teacher of chemistry at Skyline High in Oakland, California, began working on reading skills with his students, he found that students in other chemistry classes typically got weeks ahead of his class in the fall. "But I could get [my class] ahead by spring, because there was opportunity for independent learning—the text started to make sense," he stated, adding, "They [students] think, 'My eyes passed over the page, and I pronounced all the words.' They don't notice that they really didn't get it." Rather than just lecture and assign chapters for homework, Brown gives students a purpose for reading and strategies for comprehending what they are reading. When he introduces new material, the class tackles the text as a group. They grapple with the wording, graphics, and foreign terms and ask questions as they move through the reading. For example, in a unit on how atoms bond, Brown prompts his students to ponder why atoms join together and to visualize the process. He asks them to identify new and foreign terms and to determine their meaning, given the context. Given his successes, the school is training Brown's colleagues in the same techniques.

Source: Adapted from McGrath, A. (2005, February 28). A new read on teen literacy. *U.S. News and World Report, 138*(7), pp. 68–70.

Social Studies

Our goal as social studies educators and members of NCSS is to teach students the content knowledge, intellectual skills, and civic values necessary for fulfilling the duties of citizenship in a participatory democracy. NCSS—the largest association in the country devoted solely to social studies education—defines social studies as "the integrated study of the social sciences and humanities to promote civic competence" (1992, p. 1). This includes such disciplines as anthropology, archaeology, economics, geography, history, law, philosophy, political science, psychology, religion, and sociology, as well as appropriate content from the humanities, mathematics, and the natural sciences. The NCSS (1994) curriculum standards, *Expectations of Excellence: Curriculum Standards for Social Studies*, are intended to assure that an integrated social science, behavioral science, and humanities approach for achieving academic and civic competence is available to guide social studies decision makers in K–12 schools. They provide a framework to integrate other standards—national and state—in social studies, including U.S. and world history, civics and government, geography, global education, and economics.

In social studies, challenges for readers include how to navigate a wealth of factual information replete with unfamiliar names, events, and concepts. This is similar to trying to make sense of a paragraph in which all the familiar place names have been substituted with made-up or unfamiliar terms. Everyone who reads it could struggle. Many students face this trial in classrooms daily. In their attempts to absorb facts and concepts in a text, students may miss why it is to their advantage to gain insight about a time period in history or how a government functions. Vocabulary demands in social studies texts often require readers to construct meaning for concepts that are abstract. Concepts such as *imperialism, migration, culture, monarchy, socialization, opportunity cost*, and *separation of power*, for example, are open to multiple interpretations and require students to learn through a number of contexts as they refine and elaborate on their initial understandings.

Textbooks are typically used in social studies classrooms, but students are often required to read a variety of primary source documents, such as the *U.S. Declaration of Independence* and speeches by political figures. In addition, students are regularly asked to read articles from newspapers, news magazines, and other periodicals designed for elementary, middle, and high school readers. Increasingly, electronic texts—from CD-ROMs to online sources—are read in social studies classes. Students also may be required to read narrative text, including biographies, autobiographies, and fiction related to topics in history or other subjects. Whatever the source, students need to be able to differentiate factual information from opinion-laden statements and to detect bias.

Patterns of text structures in social studies can vary depending on the discipline being studied. For example, history texts usually follow a chronological approach and frequently connect information using cause and effect structures, as authors describe relationships among people, places, and events. Economics and civics texts frequently use a problem and solution or goal–action–outcome structure. Geography texts often emphasize description or compare and contrast connections, as different places and cultures are investigated and explained. Psychology and sociology texts tend to highlight key concepts using concept–definition or cause–effect connections when discussing why people behave in certain ways. Proposition–support relationships occur throughout social studies texts, as various arguments, points of view, perspectives, and interpretations are analyzed and evaluated. It is vital that teachers recognize these patterns (as authors have used them to develop text) and match instruction for students to the dominant pattern in any given reading assignment.

Visual literacy abilities also are essential. Crucial information is often presented in nonlinguistic or graphic form, including political cartoons, maps, photographs and illustrations, timelines, and data representations such as charts or tables. Comprehension is aided when students understand the purpose of these tools and have the interpretive skills necessary to decipher them.

As social studies teachers, we strive to make our classrooms places for active learning that involve student collaboration, simulations, role-playing, group inquiry projects, and so forth. Oral expression of ideas, brainstorming, and group discussion skills are key literacy needs that must be taught and learned. Implementing clearly defined discussion criteria is essential to ensuring that students understand that dialogue and debate are more than just talking. As students engage in inquiry projects—individually and in groups—they must be able to access and evaluate information from a wide range of potential sources, including electronic texts. This includes the ability to

- locate and use primary and secondary source documents
- recognize and evaluate author perspective and bias
- synthesize information from multiple sources
- make connections across chronological eras, across geographical regions, or between civic and economic issues
- present findings in a variety of forms, including oral presentations or debates and written documents that may take the form of research papers, position papers, or writing from a specific role or perspective

It is important to remember that teachers, as well as students, acquire and apply information and skills in multiple ways. We hope that you, as a literacy coach, can help social studies teachers realize that the more they learn about how literacy skills can help students unlock social studies content, the more learning can occur among their students.

STANDARD 4: Skillful Instructional Strategists

Content area literacy coaches are accomplished middle and high school teachers who are skilled in developing and implementing instructional strategies to improve academic literacy in social studies.

ELEMENT 4.1 Literacy coaches are familiar with the social studies content areas and know how reading and writing processes intersect with the disciplines included in the social studies.

Performances

4.1.1 Literacy coaches know and understand the different social sciences and humanities that are part of social studies as well as the NCSS curriculum standards and benchmarks, and how both relate to state and local student standards in social studies.

4.1.2 Literacy coaches relate adolescent development and students' linguistic and cultural backgrounds to the study of social studies content, skills, and dispositions. They share with teachers ways to tap the historical and geographical knowledge immigrant students may bring to the classroom and how to navigate different perspectives on historical events or cultural artifacts that some students from immigrant families may have.

4.1.3 Literacy coaches know the specific demands of reading social studies textbooks, including

- recognizing fact and opinion and the words that signal opinions and judgments
- distinguishing between primary and secondary sources (e.g., historical record versus textbook)
- thinking critically (e.g., drawing inferences or conclusions from facts, analyzing author's purpose and point of view, discerning cause and effect relationships, detecting bias, evaluating evidence)
- understanding the conceptual and abstract nature of vocabulary demands that require students to refine and elaborate on initial definitions
- navigating a wealth of factual information replete with unfamiliar names, events, and concepts
- using and interpreting maps, globes, and other nonlinguistic or graphic tools such as timelines, photographs, charts, statistical tables, and political cartoons
- using other text features such as glossaries, indexes, detailed databases about countries, and appendixes of documents or maps

ELEMENT 4.2 Literacy coaches demonstrate multiple comprehension strategies to assist content area teachers in developing active and competent readers within the social studies.

Performances

4.2.1 Literacy coaches know and assist social studies teachers in understanding the text structures that students encounter in social studies selections, including

- order or sequential events pattern text structure (e.g., looking for signal words; asking students to create a timeline to record events)
- cause and effect text structure (e.g., looking for signal words; asking students to make predictions and determine relationships between events; asking why people behave a certain way)
- comparison and contrast text structure (e.g., looking for signal words; asking students to record differences and similarities between people, places, or events)
- concept or definition text structure (e.g., asking students to identify what is being defined, locating the definition, and identifying the details that explain each concept)
- main idea and detail text structure (e.g., asking students to look for the topic, the main points, and supporting details)
- description text structure (e.g., asking students to identify the event, object, person, or idea being described and the corresponding supporting facts, characteristics, traits, and/or features)

- problem and solution text structure (e.g., asking students to identify the problem and possible solutions)
- goal–action–outcome text structure (e.g., asking students to identify the goal and evaluate the plan of action to accomplish that goal)
- proposition and support text structure (e.g., asking students to analyze various arguments, points of view, perspectives)

4.2.2 Literacy coaches assist social studies teachers in matching instructional methods to the dominant pattern of text structure for any given reading (e.g., developing a timeline for a reading that is organized chronologically or completing a Venn diagram for a reading that is organized in a comparison and contrast pattern).

4.2.3 Literacy coaches know and model how patterns of argument and rules of evidence are used in the social studies discipline.

4.2.4 Literacy coaches know and model strategies in order to assist social studies teachers in actively engaging students in learning, including asking students to express and defend others' viewpoints and develop and express their own informed viewpoint. Some examples of active learning strategies that promote student discussion and dialogue include visual discovery, experiential exercises, problem-solving group work, and Web quests.

4.2.5 Literacy coaches know and model strategies for interpreting maps, charts, graphs, and other nonlinguistic or graphic tools commonly used in social studies instruction.

Boston Coach Helps Teacher Make History Lessons Accessible to ELL Students

Instructional coaches in the Boston Public Schools have a very well defined role. Boston coaching components include an eight-week cycle of inquiry and study, regular demonstrations of teacher strategies in classrooms, and follow-up between the literacy coach and the individual teachers. A typical day for a coach in Boston is to meet with a teacher for one block of 80 minutes, conduct a class observation for another block, and have a meeting with an administrator for a third block. When a history teacher with a number of English-language learners spoke up about the fact that students seemed to have no idea what was going on in class—the number of concepts being taught had overwhelmed them—the coach, formerly an ESL teacher and bilingual history teacher himself, responded immediately. Over the next month, the coach helped the teacher select topics, formulate key vocabulary, gather resources beyond the textbook, and figure out instructional strategies that would help students better comprehend the history lessons. At the end of the month, changes were evident to the teacher who reflected, "Oh, now I get it. Language, language, language." The coach had succeeded in getting the teacher to think keenly about language in lesson planning and lesson delivery by, among other strategies, emphasizing key vocabulary words, securing diverse materials that link to different ability levels, and being aware of one's own language pacing and use of jargon. These changes made the history lessons more accessible to the ELLs.

Source: Adapted from Annenberg Institute for School Reform. (2005). *Coaches in the high school classroom: Studies in implementing high school reform* (Prepared for Carnegie Corporation of New York). Providence, RI: Author.

PART 3

What We Know and What We Need to Know About Literacy Coaches in Middle and High Schools: A Research Synthesis and Proposed Research Agenda

Catherine Snow, Jacy Ippolito, and Robert Schwartz
HARVARD GRADUATE SCHOOL OF EDUCATION

The standards for secondary literacy coaches presented here represent an important step toward developing a shared understanding of what coaches should be able to do and toward ensuring appropriate preparation for coaches working in middle and high schools. Since highly qualified coaches are expected to work with teachers to improve instruction, the potential of these coaching standards to promote adolescent literacy achievement is obvious. At the same time, evaluations of the coaching model or systematic study of factors affecting the implementation of coaching have not yet been carried out. The purpose of this portion of the standards is to summarize what we know and what we need to know about the coaching model focused on literacy in the secondary grades. This synthesis may help guide districts in making decisions about where coaches can function effectively and where other approaches might be more effective, and in ensuring that the conditions for successful coaching are created before coaches are hired. Given the limited empirical basis for formulating recommendations about coaching models, coaching qualifications, and procedures for preparing coaches, we hope this research synthesis and proposed research agenda will generate an interest in the systematic collection of data in those places where coaches are working in middle and high schools.

Many schools and school districts, and even a few states, have appointed literacy coaches in their efforts to promote improved literacy outcomes. Coaching also is a major new target of investment in educational improvement: The Annenberg Foundation has committed $31 million to coaching in Pennsylvania; Florida has devoted over a third of its $90 million literacy initiative to coaching; and coaching has been adopted as the model for professional development in the Boston, Dallas, New York, and Philadelphia public schools. Is this investment justified?

The coaching model being widely adopted is consistent with research evidence concerning effective professional development. That evidence suggests that local, site-specific, instructionally focused, ongoing professional development generally works better than the traditional pull-out models focused on schoolwide or districtwide issues (Guskey, 2000). The coach's role, though somewhat variable across sites, generally includes designing and implementing these preferred professional development models, by facilitating the work of ongoing collaborative teacher groups, centering the collaborative work on shared instructional challenges, promoting demonstration lessons and cross-classroom observations, and developing opportunities to inspect students' performance on tests and in-class assignments so as to inform instruction.

Thus the coaching movement very likely represents a step forward when compared to traditional investments in professional development. Nonetheless, like many good ideas in education, literacy coaching is being widely implemented based on its convergence with theory and the wisdom of practitioners, before rigorous evaluations have been carried out. Furthermore, it has been implemented in ways that vary as a function of local conditions and local understandings, with no systematic study of those variations. We simply do not yet have a blueprint of what a coach is or exactly how a coach is meant to function, so reports of success (or failure) of the coaching experiment may not be very helpful in efforts to accumulate knowledge about educational reform or to institutionalize educational improvements.

We focus on literacy because that is the work of most active coaches, although the coaching model also has been used for mathematics and social studies/history in some places. We focus on the secondary grades for several reasons: (1) because aspects of coaching in the primary grades have already been fairly well documented and studied (Walpole & McKenna, 2004); (2) because of the widespread concern about the literacy achievement of students in grades 5 and higher; and (3) because the departmentalized instruction of middle and high schools and improvement of literacy performance requires attention to reading in the content areas, creating intrinsically greater challenges for the literacy coach and more complex standards for literacy coach preparation.

The sources of information about adolescent literacy coaching are scant. We draw on the one extant review of literacy coaching in secondary schools (Sturtevant, 2003), a few local evaluations of coaching, and some portraits provided by coaches as well as by those responsible for hiring and deploying them.

What Is Secondary Literacy Coaching?

Definitions of Coaching

Although the roles and expectations of primary-grade literacy coaches have been relatively well explicated (IRA, 2004a; Walpole & McKenna, 2004), the roles and expectations of secondary literacy coaches remain less clear. Of course, this is a principal goal of the standards presented here, but other researchers and practitioners have also proffered definitions and criteria for secondary literacy coaches. Although there are commonalities among these definitions, the focus of each characterization is slightly different. Table 1 presents an attempt both to acknowledge the work that has already been done in clarifying the roles of literacy coaches and to lay the groundwork for consensus around distinguishing the core components of coaching from more peripheral aspects of the role.

It is striking that the different attempts to define coaching focus on different aspects. Walpole and McKenna (2004) discuss the various roles that coaches take; the IRA (2004a) coaching standards focus, not surprisingly, on qualifications coaches need; whereas the three discussions of secondary coaching we have found attend almost exclusively to coaching responsibilities—the tasks that coaches are meant to assume. A full definition of literacy coaching would presumably have to attend to all three of these categories, and in fact link roles, qualifications, and responsibilities in a logical fashion. We make a first attempt at that linking in the following section.

Toward a Common Definition of Literacy Coaching

In laying the groundwork for a definition of secondary literacy coaching, we make two initial distinctions: (1) between the required roles and absolutely necessary qualifications and those that would represent valuable expansions of the roles and capacities; and (2) among roles, qualifications, and responsibilities. Based on currently available descriptions of coaching and literacy-oriented professional development programs, the following set of expectations could be considered among the requisites for secondary literacy coaches:

Requisite Roles and Associated Responsibilities

- guide to improved literacy instruction
  - model instruction in teachers' classrooms
  - observe teachers and provide suggestions and feedback in one-on-one meetings (preferably before as well as after observations)
  - lead teacher inquiry groups around literacy issues
  - disseminate current literacy research findings
  - problem solve classroom dilemmas around literacy struggles

- liaison between instructional and administrative groups
  - mediate among administrative goals, teachers' goals, and students' needs
  - review local assessment data
  - help create literacy plans for schools (and perhaps individual teachers)
  - be familiar with a variety of formal and informal assessments
  - prepare feedback for administrators, teachers, and perhaps students documenting changes in students' literacy achievement

Requisite Qualifications

- strong foundation in literacy
  - credentials and/or experience in literacy instruction, literacy assessment, as well as literacy acquisition processes and problems in literacy development

- strong leadership skills
- familiarity with adult learning
  - knowledge of how to work with teachers and how to foster an atmosphere of inquiry

Table 1. Currently Available Definitions of Coaching (Both Primary and Secondary)

Sources	Coaches' Roles	Coaches' Qualifications	Coaches' Responsibilities
		Primary School Focus	
Walpole, S., & McKenna, M.C. (2004). *The literacy coach's handbook: A guide to research-based practice.* New York: Guilford.	• Learner • Grant writer • School-level planner • Curriculum expert • Researcher • Teacher • School leader (pp. 1–20)		
International Reading Association (IRA). (2004a). *The role and qualifications of the reading coach in the United States* (Position statement). Newark, DE: Author.		• Excellent classroom teacher • Familiarity with student age group • In-depth knowledge of reading processes, acquisition, assessment, and instruction • Experience working with teachers to improve their practices • Excellent presenter (preferably with experience presenting at conferences and to groups of teachers) • Experience or preparation that enables [the mastery of the] complexities of observing and modeling in classrooms and providing feedback to teachers (pp. 3–4)	
Neufeld, B., & Roper, D. (2003). *Coaching: A strategy for developing instructional capacity—Promises and practicalities* (Prepared for The Aspen Institute Program on Education and The Annenberg Institute for School Reform). Cambridge, MA: Education Matters.		• Skillful with adult learners • Flexible • Able to determine teachers' needs	• Help teachers improve instruction • Help teachers transfer what they learn about new practices to their classrooms • Help establish a safe environment in which teachers can strive to improve their practice without fear of negative criticism or evaluation • Help teachers develop leadership skills with which they can support the work of their colleagues • Provide small-group professional development sessions for teachers (pp. 7–10)

Sources	Coaches' Roles	Coaches' Qualifications	Coaches' Responsibilities
		Secondary School Focus	
Sturtevant, E.G. (2003). *The literacy coach: A key to improving teaching and learning in secondary schools.* Washington, DC: Alliance for Excellent Education.			• Lead literacy teams (that then review assessment data and develop literacy plans for the school) • Guide teachers in using appropriate strategies • Liaise with teachers and administrators • Be regarded as expert teachers (pp. 18–19)
Greenleaf, C., Katz, M., & Schoenbach, R. (2001, April). *Close readings: The impact of case inquiry on secondary teachers' literacy knowledge and practice and student achievement.* Paper presented at the annual meeting of the American Educational Research Association, Seattle, WA.			• Establish a Strategic Literacy Initiative/Network • Lead generative professional development—ongoing professional development work where teachers support each others' growth (p. 6) • Provide sustained professional development for site-based interdisciplinary teams of teachers (p. 7) • Promote group reflection on own literacy practices and responses as a way into helping students with their practices (p. 10) • Provide access to experientially rich demonstrations of specific teaching approaches (p. 55)
Grossman, P., Wineburg, S., & Woolworth, S. (2000). *What makes teacher community different from a gathering of teachers* (No. O-00-1). Seattle, WA: Center for the Study of Teaching and Policy, Center on English Learning & Achievement.			• Support continual intellectual development of teachers (in small communities) (p. 14) • Implement distributed cognition—learning from colleagues and relying on colleagues (pp. 32–33)

Note. This table does not represent an exhaustive review of currently available definitions of secondary literacy coaching. Instead, its aim is to capture some frequently cited sources for role definition.

- familiarity with the target student age groups
- skilled classroom teacher

This short list of requisites is composed of items that seem to crop up again and again in the literature as necessary for successful coaching. But there are a few additional expectations that appear once or twice in the literature or in reports from knowledgeable coaches that, although perhaps not crucial enough to be listed as requisites, would clearly enhance a coach's functioning. We have termed these aspects *discretionary roles*, *associated responsibilities*, and *discretionary qualifications*.

Discretionary Roles and Associated Responsibilities

- grant writer
  - identify opportunities for fundraising
  - identify school needs around which to fundraise
  - formulate strong documents
- school-level planner
  - schedule classes, organize literacy blocks
  - schedule professional development time and common planning time for teachers
- advisor to administration
  - help write school improvement plans
  - plan school and community events around literacy
- mediator between school and community literacy efforts
  - work with parents
  - recruit and provide roles for local organizations
- researcher
  - consume current literacy research
  - collect teacher- and student-level data
  - write research-oriented reports and program evaluations
  - recruit and work with academic research partners

Discretionary Qualifications

- credentials and/or experience in specific content areas in which literacy coaching may take place (e.g., English language arts, mathematics, science, social studies)
- strong personal literacy and communication skills
- excellent presentation skills
- excellent interpersonal skills

This list can hardly be considered prescriptive. Instead, it is an initial guide based on the collective wisdom of those who have already begun implementing coaching programs. It is clearly a rather long list of crucial and of desirable qualifications. Its length makes clear why some might worry that many already appointed coaches are not functioning at the high level that the coaching model presupposes. More optimistically, it suggests what characteristics those hiring coaches should look for, as well as the domains and capabilities that programs of professional preparation and/or development for coaches need to address.

Challenges to Being a Secondary Literacy Coach

What are the major differences between a literacy coach working in the primary grades and one working in a middle or high school environment? The differences are seen most clearly when looking at the scope of the jobs, the teachers being coached, and the literacy needs of students at the primary and secondary grade levels.

The scope of the literacy coach role is markedly different at the primary and secondary levels. Coaches working at both levels are expected to focus their attention on improving teachers' literacy instruction; however, coaches working with primary-grade teachers may have a bit more traction, as they are typically working with only a small group of teachers, with teachers who have some training in literacy instruction, and with teachers who interact with their own students for entire days. Thus coaches leading inquiry groups or literacy teams in the primary grades are working with professionals who all see teaching reading and writing as a central facet of their jobs. Moreover, literacy blocks in the primary grades are frequently longer than those in upper grades (up to 120 minutes), can be extended beyond the scheduled time if necessary, and are held daily—a reflection of the general agreement that teaching children to read is the most important task of the primary grades. Thus the primary-grade literacy coach contributes expertise in the domain teachers and their supervisors value most highly and attend to most diligently.

Coaches at the primary level are also often expected to carry out administrative duties such as scheduling literacy blocks, linking between the principal and the primary-grade team of teachers, and coordinating primary-grade assessment efforts. Some sources even suggest that primary-grade coaches should have enough time to apply for grants, carry out small research projects, as well as continue to provide ongoing professional development sessions for teachers (Walpole & McKenna, 2004).

The large scope of the primary literacy coach's role may in part stem from the fact that a great deal is known about how to successfully teach reading and writing to primary-grade children. Coaches and teachers at these levels are focusing on helping children understand the alphabetic principle, decode print, attend to new vocabulary, and comprehend relatively simple stories and nonfiction pieces. There are well-disseminated pedagogical procedures for achieving these goals. Furthermore, standard curricula provide considerable support to teachers in planning and sequencing primary literacy instruction. When a knowledgeable primary-grade coach enters a school with willing kindergarten through third-grade teachers who all see their jobs as mostly teaching literacy, a rich literacy environment can be quickly established and nourished.

In contrast, a secondary-grade literacy coach faces a number of unique challenges. First, literacy coaches working in sixth grade and beyond are often dealing with larger numbers of teachers housed in several content area departments. Teachers at these grade levels may no longer see teaching reading and writing as one of their primary roles as a teacher; instead, these teachers are mainly focused on communicating specific content area knowledge and skills (Sturtevant, 2003). Consider a 10th-grade trigonometry teacher who sees five or six classes of 25 students every day. Her focus is helping her students to parse the relationships between angles, enclosed two-dimensional figures, and their connection to real-world problems. Although every content area teacher is teaching a specific way of reading the world, these teachers may not view their role as having to do with inculcating literacy skills per se. This lack of awareness of the literacy needs of their students poses a challenge for the secondary-grade literacy coach.

Complicating matters further, students in sixth grade and beyond come to school with a wider variety both of literacy skills and of literacy deficits than students in the earlier grades (RAND Reading Study Group, 2002). In a sixth-grade classroom, for instance, there may be a small group of students reading and writing at a high school level, whereas there may be another small group of students who still find decoding difficult. Sixth graders who struggle with content area texts may need instruction or intervention in word reading, fluency, vocabulary, inferencing skills, attention to text features, study skills, and/or in strategic reading. Finding themselves on the other side of the "learn to read, read to learn" divide (Chall, 1992), students in the middle and upper grades can be overwhelmed by the multiple comprehension demands of the various content areas. Moving from science, to social studies, to mathematics, to English language arts, and then to foreign language and arts classes, students can more easily slip through the literacy "cracks," with no single teacher being able to monitor student progress across a full day or to provide consistent accommodations and literacy support.

> Moving from science, to social studies, to mathematics, to English language arts, and then to foreign language and arts classes, students can more easily slip through the literacy "cracks," with no single teacher being able to monitor student progress across a full day or to provide consistent accommodations and literacy support.

All of this points to a challenging job for secondary literacy coaches. Coaches leading inquiry groups around literacy issues may meet with a fair bit of resistance from teachers who feel that focusing on literacy is taking away from time spent on honing content area skills, or that the professional development literacy coaches provide is irrelevant to them. As Sturtevant (2003) states, "Compounding the problem is that many content area teachers do not believe that they should include literacy-related strategies in their repertoire of teaching practices" (p. 10). Thus the two-fold problem arises of how to persuade teachers in middle school and beyond that teaching literacy remains a priority, and how to help the teachers incorporate literacy instruction into their already overflowing curriculum calendars. Furthermore, coaches at the secondary level may experience isolation from their colleagues, not feeling part of any one department and holding neither teacher nor administrative status. Though literacy coaches at all levels may find it difficult to float among teacher, coach, and administrative roles, a secondary coach may feel particularly estranged from both teacher and administrative roles due to the departmentalization of subject area teaching in middle school and beyond. Also, secondary coaches are working under very strict time constraints, often in the 45- to 60-minute time blocks allowed for classes. This time crunch creates an additional challenge for helping content area teachers to communicate both good literacy practices and content area knowledge to large numbers of students.

Last, research has generated inadequate knowledge about how best to respond to the wide range of literacy needs of older students. There is a great deal of literature reflecting on the contextualized benefits of particular literacy practices in the secondary grades; however, there is a dearth of empirical research demonstrating how particular literacy instructional practices improve older students' outcomes across a variety of contexts. Though faced with a wider skill range among students, a wider array of problems among the struggling readers and writers, and a generally lower level of motivation among adolescents experiencing the effects of past failures and competing social pressures, secondary coaches simply have fewer proven strategies to apply. Furthermore, given the wide array of literacy challenges older readers might face, unrealistic demands might well be placed on coaches to help teachers address problems in the classroom that should actually be addressed with intensive student-focused interventions. Secondary coaches may also need to assume the responsibility of educating administrators and teachers about the need for differentiated instruction that includes options for intervention delivered outside the regular classroom, for students substantially behind their peers in reading level. In other words, the presence in a middle or high school of a coach focused on professional development to improve literacy instruction does not eliminate the need for reading specialists or others focused on the needs of readers with disabilities or severe delays.

We do not mean to suggest that the situation is hopeless, nor that primary-grade coaches lead luxurious, stress-free lives while secondary coaches are unsung heroes toiling away to little effect. Coaches at all levels are more similar than they are different, working in difficult "in-between" jobs that require interpersonal skills, teaching skills, and a great deal of literacy knowledge. It is important, though, as we move into an era where coaching is being adopted ever more aggressively as the solution to the literacy problems of middle and high school students, to recognize the specific challenges the coaching model faces at those levels.

Coaching as a Vehicle for Professional Development

Having reviewed some of the challenges faced by secondary literacy coaches, it is important to outline briefly a way in which these coaches might broadly define their roles in a positive way. How should coaches conceive of their roles? On a daily basis, when they may be alternately pushed and pulled back and forth into teacher and administrator roles, how can coaches keep their minds set on a particular path that lies somewhere in between?

One answer, broadly speaking, might be for literacy coaches to envision themselves as vehicles for professional development. A literacy coach working at any grade level is more concerned with teachers' learning and growth than with students' learning and growth. Whereas reading specialists or learning disability specialists typically spend most of their time working with students and only a small portion of time focused on staff development, most literacy coaches are primarily concerned with increasing the skills and knowledge of teachers and administrators. Therefore, most coaches are operating mainly as site-based, ongoing professional developers.

This may not be a shocking revelation; however, by thinking of literacy coaches as vehicles for professional development, rather than as elevated classroom teachers or reading specialists, a new set of guidelines for the coaching role can be defined. Research and conventional wisdom around best practices for professional development can suddenly be applied to models for literacy coaching. Providing an in-depth analysis of connections between professional development literature and literacy coaching roles and expectations is not the focus of this piece, yet one example of how professional development literature might provide a basis for further defining coaching is given below.

Guskey (2000) outlines four common elements found in most successful professional development initiatives: "A clear focus on learning and learners, an emphasis on individual and organizational change, small changes guided by a grand vision, and ongoing professional development that is procedurally embedded" (pp. 36–38). We would be remiss in talking about Guskey's work without mentioning his emphasis on the necessity of designing and implementing evaluations of professional development efforts.

Guskey suggests a model for professional development evaluation that includes five levels of evaluation:

1. participants' reactions
2. participants' learning
3. organization support and change
4. participants' use of new knowledge and skills
5. student learning outcomes

To adequately collect, analyze, and report data at each of these five levels is no small undertaking; however, an evaluation system that touches each of these areas is a worthwhile goal for schools and districts wishing to appraise their burgeoning coaching programs.

Clearly this is just one example of how knowledge from professional development literature could influence the definitions, roles, and evaluations of coaching models, yet it demonstrates the potential power of conceiving of secondary literacy coaches as vehicles for professional development. Thinking of coaches in this way cannot ensure a successful literacy coaching program; nonetheless, this perspective could be a useful way of presenting coaching to teachers, administrators, policymakers, and others to ensure that the goals and guidelines of coaching programs consistently focus on staff development. Though student learning and growth are the eventual goals of all coaching programs, the immediate need is to focus the coach's role on adult learning.

How Do Coaches Fit Into the Larger Organizational Systems of Schools and Districts?

What We Know From Successful Implementations About School/District Support

In the domain of the coach's institutional fit, as in the others we have discussed, our knowledge base consists primarily of case studies and practitioner reports rather than systematic study. Indeed, educational researchers have not produced the tools that would be needed to monitor contextual factors in schools and school districts that might be related to the success of coaching.

It is clear, though, that districts where coaching has taken hold as a primary channel for the delivery of professional development have been characterized by district leaders' public commitment to the coaching model and by the provision of resources so that schools could hire well-prepared coaches. In Boston, Massachusetts, the coaches were first introduced and supported by the Boston Plan for Excellence (BPE), an organization designed to support the work of Boston Public Schools but outside its organizational structure. Because of the support from the BPE, the initial experiences schools had with coaches were positive, and the model spread throughout the district accompanied by a good reputation and an eagerness to embrace it. Nonetheless, Boston Public Schools faces the constant challenge of recruiting and retaining well-prepared coaches, especially in secondary grades. And coaches working in Boston, who typically divide their time between two schools, often note that their level of effectiveness in one school is greater than in another, reflecting differences in school organizational structure.

Managing Institutional Receptiveness

While there is to our knowledge no systematic study of how coaches should and do fit into the organizational structure of schools, it is clear that the coach–school interface can be complex. First, the administrative role of coaches can be ambiguous. If they are seen by teachers as part of the administration and as tools in a teacher-assessment agenda, then their potential to support improvements in instruction will be constrained, and an oppositional relationship between teachers and coaches can easily emerge. If they are, on the other hand, seen primarily as allies of the teachers, perhaps even as allies in opposition to the administration, their role as instructional leaders and their authority to guide change can also be undermined. If the institutional role of the coaches is ambiguous, then they run the risk of becoming irrelevant to the real work of the school.

> Many coaches operate in ways that improve the functioning of schools and that serve the needs of administration, teaching staff, and ultimately students.

Many coaches operate in ways that improve the functioning of schools and that serve the needs of administration, teaching staff, and ultimately students. But it is not inconceivable that the introduction of a coach into a school organization could end up causing more harm than good (e.g., by undermining a fragile relationship of trust between principal and teachers, by threatening the emergence of teacher responsibility for student learning, or by creating a situation that undermines the coach's intended role by using the coach as a reading specialist directly responsible for helping failing students rather than as someone responsible for professional development). We need to know more about how to judge schools as organizations along the dimensions of trust, responsibility, and readiness for change, so as to have some metric for evaluating the impact of introducing coaching into the full array of schools that exist.

What Do We Need to Know to Move Forward?

Research on Coaching

Ideally, before hiring new secondary literacy coaches, schools and districts would be able to consult a solid body of empirical research suggesting whether secondary literacy coaches are effective and what array of factors influences their effectiveness. Unfortunately, given the current demands of No Child Left Behind policies and the ever-present achievement gap in middle and high schools around the United States, waiting for that body of research to be produced before committing to coaching is neither feasible nor wise. Schools and districts around the country are already hiring new coaches and charging them with closing the achievement gap and raising students' performance on high-stakes tests (specifically English language arts scores, but also scores in other content areas such as mathematics, science, and social studies). Given the rapid growth of coaching as both a vehicle for professional development and as an instrument for improving student performance, we argue that a different kind of research agenda must be adopted in looking at secondary literacy coaches—one that starts with the practice as it exists and addresses questions of greatest importance to the practitioners, while at the same time attending to possibilities for accumulating findings across sites (see Donovan, Wigdor, & Snow, 2003, for a more extended description of this kind of research agenda).

> Given the rapid growth of coaching as both a vehicle for professional development and as an instrument for improving student performance, we argue that a different kind of research agenda must be adopted in looking at secondary literacy coaches—one that starts with the practice as it exists and addresses questions of greatest importance to the practitioners, while at the same time attending to possibilities for accumulating findings across sites.

Ideally, districts and states that are introducing coaches on a large scale would do so in a way that allowed for some inferences about their effectiveness (e.g., ranking schools on performance and then randomly assigning coaches initially to half the schools at each performance level, and monitoring student performance in subsequent years in both sets of schools). In an evaluation like this, a number of outcome variables could be used as a basis for inferring the value of the coaching model: student performance on researcher-designed and/or state accountability assessments, teacher satisfaction with the coaches and the coaching model, teacher retention, district expenditures on professional development, and so on.

If a design that allows for evaluation of impact is impractical for political or other reasons, then considerable useful information about coaching can still be acquired. Careful observational studies of the coaches' activities would generate descriptive data about the coaching model adhered to and the quality of its implementation. Student performance would, of course, be charted at the school level, ideally longitudinally as well as cross-sectionally. Teacher and administrator surveys could be administered before the placement of coaches, to determine baselines for dimensions of institutional trust, satisfaction with professional development, satisfaction with the literacy program, and so on. Those contextual factors would then help researchers interpret differences among schools in effectiveness of the coaching model as indicated by changes in student performance and in teacher satisfaction with their experiences in coaching sessions.

In the absence of the capacity or will to engage in this sort of systematic study of variation across schools in coaching implementation and outcomes, much can still be learned from case studies of coaches, both those who successfully implement site-based professional development and those who encounter resistance or opposition.

We started Part 3 by noting that good ideas in education often fail to take hold because they are implemented without sufficient attention to the conditions under which they might operate optimally and be institutionalized. Similarly, there is an unfortunate tendency for educational researchers to engage in research that is not directly relevant to decisions about practice. We are arguing here for a practice-embedded research agenda that would both improve the value of good ideas like coaching to the educational institutions that wish to implement them, and that would enable the field to learn from the experience of trying out those good ideas. Coaching in middle and high schools is ripe to be the site of such a revolutionary approach to educational research.

There are also many questions about coaching that go beyond the relatively straightforward ones related to impact:

- In what domains is the impact of literacy coaches greatest? Student learning, teacher learning, and school climate are all domains where impact might be expected. If impacts are found, can they be measured in all three of these areas? Is degree of impact in one of them related to impact in the others?

- How can schools begin to collect their own data about the effects of literacy coaching? What information should they be paying attention to (and sharing with research partners)?

- How can we compare literacy coaches across contexts if schools are using coaches very differently (e.g., directing their efforts primarily to English language arts teachers versus teachers dealing with a particular group of students, providing some services directly to students versus exclusively to teachers, working with several schools or with only one)? What is the full array of responsibilities appropriately assumed by coaches in different school and district settings?

- What are the characteristics of highly effective coaches? What professional qualifications, prior experiences, and training are related to success in the coaching role?

- What is the relationship between coaches' familiarity with content area standards and effective integration of literacy instruction into content area lessons?

- Do coaches with a great deal of content area knowledge threaten content area teachers' sense of expertise? Or are coaches with a great deal of content area knowledge more easily accepted into content area classrooms?

- What reading comprehension strategies and practices are best received by the various content area teachers?

- Which comprehension strategies and practices are most effective for students in the various content area classes?

- How often, and in what size groups, should coaches and content area teachers meet to plan and evaluate instruction?

- How do coach-led teacher teams divide and share their time regarding literacy and content area instruction?

- What differences between content area teachers' practices can be attributed to participation in coach-led teacher meetings?

Secondary Literacy Coaches of the Future: What Training Programs Should Consider

Just a few years ago, most literacy-oriented degree and training programs focused almost exclusively on training reading specialists. These reading specialists were being prepared mostly to work in the primary grades with beginning and struggling readers. As a result, the programs concentrated on teaching future reading specialists about the earliest stages of literacy development and the challenges typically faced by beginning readers.

Now, literacy-oriented degree and training programs are starting to respond to the way in which many former reading specialists are actually being used in districts nationwide. Many teachers who completed master's programs in reading have gone on to become literacy coaches, spending an increasing amount of time working with teachers as opposed to students. This may be the case even more so for middle and high school reading specialists, who instead of seeing only a handful of students out of the hundreds that might attend a large middle or high school are being asked to coach content area teachers in an effort to incorporate effective literacy instruction into all classrooms. Literacy-oriented degree and training programs are responding to this phenomenon in two ways: (1) They are using the term "literacy coach" more frequently, paying closer attention to the similarities and differences between the roles of reading specialists and literacy coaches. (2) They are acknowledging that both reading specialists and literacy coaches are working with adolescent and adult readers as well as with beginning readers; therefore, there is a need for classroom and practicum experiences that focus on working with middle and high school students as well as working with staff.

Here we offer some initial suggestions about what these training programs might consider as they develop and expand their offerings for teachers wishing to become secondary literacy coaches:

Consideration of Entrance Qualifications

- Programs training secondary literacy coaches will need to consider the qualifications of their applicants carefully. Whereas programs training reading specialists once upon a time admitted students with little to no teaching experience, many now require a minimum number of years of teaching experience. Programs training literacy coaches should probably follow suit, taking only applicants who will be seen by peers and future colleagues as highly skilled teachers as well as coaches. Though there may be exceptions—cases where coaches have been highly effective despite having little previous classroom teaching experience—the majority of future coaches will need to have a classroom background in order to win the confidence and respect of the teachers they will be coaching.

> The majority of future coaches will need to have a classroom background in order to win the confidence and respect of the teachers they will be coaching.

- Besides past classroom teaching experience, some attention might be given to the variety of past educational experiences applicants will bring into a training program. Are teachers who have backgrounds teaching middle and high school automatically more prepared to become coaches for those grade levels? Are teachers in certain subject areas better equipped to be coaches for those subject areas (e.g., a science teacher being a better literacy coach for other science teachers)? Might someone with a background in adolescent psychology or in adult development be better prepared to become a literacy coach for middle and high school teachers? Future research efforts should be able to help training programs make some of these distinctions.

Consideration of Practicum Experiences

- Practicum experiences in many reading specialist programs focus exclusively on working with small groups of students (if not individuals), and mostly at younger ages. Programs for literacy coaches (particularly secondary literacy coaches) need to be much broader—including experiences working with a variety of content area teachers and adolescent students. Moreover, secondary literacy coach programs need to help match aspiring coaches with current coach mentors so that there are ample apprenticeship opportunities. Future coaches need opportunities to witness firsthand the navigation among teacher, coach, and administrative roles that they will soon face themselves.

Consideration of Literacy and Content Area Knowledge

- The course content delivered to future secondary literacy coaches needs not only to include information about the development of literacy skills, but it also needs to focus on the challenges that face adolescents, ELLs, learning-disabled students, and struggling adult readers. Comprehension, vocabulary, fluency, motivational challenges, and instructional strategies need to be at the heart of secondary literacy coach training programs.

- In addition to a broader focus on the literacy needs of older students, attention needs to be given to adult education. Because literacy coaches at all levels are working mostly with adults, it makes sense to spend time both in courses and in practicum experiences exploring the nature of adult learning and development.
- Last, more attention needs to be given to the importance of a literacy coach's command of content area knowledge. Some course or practicum experience exploring literacy across content areas seems like a basic requirement for future secondary literacy coaches.

Again, these are just a few of the most important concerns facing literacy-oriented degree and training programs. Over the next five years, as the demand for secondary literacy coaches grows, we can only hope that the degree and training programs from which they are acquiring their qualifications invest in discovering the best ways to prepare coaches for their roles.

Conclusion

Coaching is an approach to literacy reform that is attracting increasing interest from districts and funders. It has been implemented most widely in the primary grades, but is spreading to the secondary grades. The IRA standards for secondary literacy coaches represent a first step toward defining the qualifications that coaches need, but by themselves they deal with only one aspect of the new challenges that extension creates. The coaching model seems well designed to improve both teacher professional development and student literacy outcomes. We believe that the coaching model has great potential, but note that it is being adopted widely, in some places with the investment of a great deal of money; in a variety of ways; and without provision for the systematic collection of data about its effectiveness, about conditions that would facilitate coaching success, or about the best methods to prepare coaches. We hope Part 3 has clarified some of the challenges associated with using coaches effectively, so as to motivate districts and schools to engage in a systematic study of how they are using coaches and what the consequences of coaching are for students, teachers, and districts.

References

ACT. (2003, October 1). Teachers are less likely to teach important reading skills to some high school students than to others [Press release]. Iowa City, IA: Author.

Allington, R. (1994). The schools we have. The schools we need. *The Reading Teacher, 48*(1), 14–29.

American Association for Advancement of Science. (1993). *Benchmarks for science literacy* (Project 2061). New York: Oxford University Press.

American Diploma Project. (2004). *Ready or not: Creating a high school diploma that counts*. Washington, DC: Achieve, Inc. Available: http://www.achieve.org/achieve.nsf/AmericanDiplomaProject

Annenberg Institute for School Reform. (2005). *Coaches in the high school classroom: Studies in implementing high school reform* (Prepared for Carnegie Corporation of New York). Providence, RI: Author.

Arenson, K.W. (2005, August 31). SAT math scores at record high, but those on the verbal exam are stagnant. *The New York Times*, p. 16.

Artley, S. (1944). A study of certain relationships existing between general reading comprehension and reading comprehension in a specific subject matter area. *Journal of Educational Research, 37*(6), 464–473.

Biancarosa, G., & Snow, C. (2004). *Reading next: A vision for action and research in middle and high school literacy*. Washington, DC: Alliance for Education.

Chall, J. (1992). The new reading debates: Evidence from science, art and ideology. *Teachers College Record, 94*(2), 315–328.

Darling-Hammond, L., & McLaughlin, M. (1995). Policies that support professional development in an era of reform. *Phi Delta Kappan, 76*(8), 597–604.

DiVesta, F.J., Hayward, K.G., & Orlando, V.P. (1979). Developmental trends in monitoring for comprehension. *Child Development, 50*, 97–105.

Donovan, M.S., Wigdor, A.K., & Snow, C.E. (Eds.). (2003). *Strategic education research partnership*. Washington, DC: National Academies Press.

Garet, M.S., Porter, A.C., Desimone, L., Birman, B.F., & Yoon, K.S. (2001). What makes professional development effective? Results from a national sample of teachers. *American Educational Research Journal, 38*(4), 915–945. Available: http://aztla.asu.edu/ProfDev1.pdf

Graduation for All Act, H.R. 547, 109th Cong., 1st Sess. (2005).

Greenleaf, C., Katz, M., & Schoenbach, R. (2001, April). *Close readings: The impact of case inquiry on secondary teachers' literacy knowledge and practice and student achievement*. Paper presented at the annual meeting of the American Educational Research Association, Seattle, WA.

Grossman, P., Wineburg, S., & Woolworth, S. (2000). *What makes teacher community different from a gathering of teachers* (No. O-00-1). Seattle, WA: Center for the Study of Teaching and Policy, Center on English Learning & Achievement.

Guskey, T.R. (2000). *Evaluating professional development*. Thousand Oaks, CA: Corwin Press.

International Reading Association (IRA). (2004a). *The role and qualifications of the reading coach in the United States* (Position statement). Newark, DE: Author. Available: http://www.reading.org/downloads/positions/ps1065_reading_coach.pdf

International Reading Association (IRA). (2004b). *Standards for reading professionals—Revised 2003*. Newark, DE: Author. Available: http://www.reading.org/resources/issues/reports/professional_standards.html

International Reading Association (IRA) & National Council of Teachers of English (NCTE). (1996). *Standards for the English language arts*. Newark, DE; Urbana, IL: Authors.

Irakson, R.L., & Miller, J.W. (1978). Sensitivity to syntactic and semantic cues in good and poor comprehenders. *Journal of Educational Psychology, 68*, 787–792.

Joftus, S. (2002). *Every child a graduate: A framework for an excellent education for all middle and high school students*. Washington, DC: Alliance for Excellent Education.

Joyce, B., & Showers, B. (1996). Staff development as a comprehensive service organization. *Journal of Staff Development, 17*(1), 2–6.

Kamil, M.L. (2003). *Adolescents and literacy: Reading for the 21st century*. Washington, DC: Alliance for Excellent Education. Available: http://www.all4ed.org/publications/AdolescentsAndLiteracy.pdf

Kinsella, K. (2001). Reading Strategies Series (Language Arts, Mathematics, Science, Social Studies). Parsippany, NJ: Pearson Education.

Manzo, K.K. (2005, February 16). Dynamic duo. *Education Week, 24*(23), pp. 37–39.

Matsuura, K. (2002, September 8). Message from the Director-General of UNESCO on the occasion of International Literacy Day. Available: http://portal.unesco.org/education/en/ev.php-URL_ID = 4847&URL_DO = DO_TOPIC&URL_SECTION = 201.html

McGrath, A. (2005, February 28). A new read on teen literacy. *U.S. News and World Report, 138*(7), pp. 68–70.

National Association of Secondary School Principals (NASSP). (2005). *Creating a culture of literacy: A guide for middle and high school principals*. Reston, VA: Author.

National Council for the Social Studies (NCSS). (1992). *A vision of powerful teaching and learning in the social studies: Building social understanding and civic efficacy*. Silver Spring, MD: Author.

National Council for the Social Studies (NCSS). (1994). *Expectations of excellence: Curriculum standards for social studies*. Silver Spring, MD: Author.

National Council of Teachers of Mathematics (NCTM). (2000). *Principles and standards for school mathematics*. Reston, VA: Author. Available: http://standards.nctm.org/document/chapter1/index.htm; Introduction

National Institute of Child Health and Human Development (NICHD). (2000). *Report of the National Reading Panel. Teaching children to read: An evidence-based assessment of the scientific research literature on reading and its implications for reading instruction* (NIH Publication No. 00-4769). Washington, DC: U.S. Government Printing Office. Available: http://www.nichd.nih.gov/publications/nrp/small book.htm

National Research Council. (1996). *National science education standards*. Washington, DC: National Academy Press.

Neufeld, B., & Roper, D. (2003). *Coaching: A strategy for developing instructional capacity—Promises and practicalities* (Prepared for The Aspen Institute Program on Education and The Annenberg Institute for School Reform). Cambridge, MA: Education Matters.

Ogle, D.M. (1986). K-W-L: A teaching model that develops active reading of expository text. *The Reading Teacher, 39*(6), 564–570.

Owings, R.A., Peterson, G.A., Bransford, J.D., Morris, C.D., & Stein, B.S. (1980). Spontaneous monitoring and regulations of learning: A comparison of successful and less successful fifth graders. *Journal of Educational Psychology, 72*, 250–256.

Palincsar, A.S., & Brown, A.L. (1984). Reciprocal teaching of comprehension-fostering and comprehension-monitoring activities. *Cognition and Instruction, 2*, 117–175.

PASS Act, S.1061, 109th Cong., 1st Sess. (2005).

Peterson, C.L., Caverly, D.C., Nicholson, S.A., O'Neal, S., & Cusenbary, S. (2001). *Building reading proficiency at the secondary level*. Austin, TX: Southwest Educational Development Laboratory.

RAND Reading Study Group. (2002). *Reading for understanding: Toward an R&D program in reading comprehension*. Santa Monica, CA: RAND. Available: http://www.rand.org/multi/achievement forall/reading/readreport.html

Russo, A. (2004, July/August). School-based coaching: A revolution in professional development—or just the latest fad? *Harvard Education Letter* [Online]. Available: http://www.edletter.org/past/issues/2004-ja/coaching.shtml

Smith, H.K. (1967). The responses of good and poor readers when asked to read for different purposes. *Reading Research Quarterly, 3*, 53–84.

Stauffer, R.B. (1969). *Teaching reading as a thinking process*. New York: Harper.

Sturtevant, E.G. (2003). *The literacy coach: A key to improving teaching and learning in secondary schools*. Washington, DC: Alliance for Excellent Education.

Symonds, K.W. (2003). *Literacy coaching: How school districts can support a long-term strategy in a short-term world*. Oakland, CA: Bay Area School Reform Collaborative.

Their, M., & Daviss, B. (2002). *The new science literacy*. Portsmouth, NH: Heinemann.

Toll, C.A. (2005). *The literacy coach's survival guide: Essential questions and practical answers*. Newark, DE: International Reading Association.

Walpole, S., & McKenna, M.C. (2004). *The literacy coach's handbook: A guide to research-based practice*. New York: Guilford.